Welcome to our third collection!

For years the idea of a humor collection floated around the Athens Writers Association. It seemed a natural fit for a writing group, for residents of a southern town (we know southerners *have* to have a sense of humor to put up with this heat), and a nice change of pace from the more serious subjects of our first two collections, *Writers After Dark*, and *The Journey Home*.

I volunteered to lead an esteemed group of editors in putting together our long-planned collection. Only then did I learn the joke was on me; what I'd presumed would be an *easier* subject matter in fact led to the most challenging collection we'd ever put together.

Good writing is by no means universally agreed upon but good comedy almost calls for universal *disagreement*. There must be surprise, wonder, a new take, a clever angle – something different than straight-up storytelling – and that unusualness often delights and befuddles people in equal measure. I sat across from colleagues formally considered sane, astute, and reliable and plotted whether I could reach the butterfly net in time to subdue them for their insane taste in submissions. I also got concerned looks as I tried to explain for five minutes how something could be hilarious just because it was bizarre (so you can blame me for the bizarre piece).

But, just as with egg juggling, a great challenge often ends in comic gold. The thirty-three pieces in this collection are often askew and unusual, as well as sweet, cute, and clever, and are sure to illicit both LOLs and WTFs. We have included a wide sampling because everyone's sense of humor is as unique as they are, and everyone will have a different favorite.

In the end, I loved how much variety, imagination, and boldness these writers put into their work and I hope you will have as much fun reading our comedy collection as we had putting it together. I came away with a whole new respect for comedy writers, as well as

i

a burning desire to edit *Laughin' in Athens: Volume 2* – just kidding!

Best wishes,
Katherine Cerulean, Athens Writers Association founder

P.S. Special thanks to my partners in crime, the other editors, for all the time, effort, and hard work they put toward this collection, and *extra* special thanks to Jenny Innes for designing our wonderful cover and writing the copy for it.

The Athens Writers Association
presents

Laughin' in Athens

Edited by
Katherine Cerulean
Jill Hartmann-Roberts
Jennifer Innes
Rob White

Laughin' in Athens

Cover design and copy by Jennifer Innes

Copyright © Athens Writers Association 2017

All rights reserved. No part of this publication may be reproduced or transmitted in any form or by any means, electronic or mechanical, including photocopy, recording, or any information storage and retrieval system, without the prior written permission of the author.

ISBN-13: 978-1548388676

ISBN-10: 154838867X

athenswritersassociation.wordpress.com

Founder's Message i
The Tall Modern Tale of a Small 80s Boy by Rob White 9
Social Grammar by Alan Curtis 12
Just My Type by Michelle Correll 13
Canned Heat by A C (Shorty) Wilmoth 14
Luckiest Cat by Alia Ghosheh 19
Absurdist by Sam Lane 20
The Dance by Larry Coleman 21
For Your Convenience by Katherine Cerulean 23
A Gardener's Rap by Zhanna P. Rader 30
Auguste Rodin's "The Thinker" by Zhanna P. Rader 32
Spindles of Life by Jim Murdock 33
Too Many Chicken Dinners? by Shantala Kay Russell 37
College by Chelsea Brooks 38
Is God a Border Collie? by Genie Smith Bernstein 39
The Night Stalker by Robert Alan Black, Ph.D 42
The Secrets Her Hair Could Not Hide by Alia Ghosheh ... 50
A Writer's Life by Daniel (Denny) Galt 52
Creation Theory by Teresa Friedlander 53
Toilet Humor by Sam Lane 55
No Country for Fat Tires by Kathryn Kyker 56
Holiday Smells by Chelsea Brooks 62
Limericks by Zhanna P. Rader 63
So You Want to Be a Demon Hunter: A Beginner's Guide to

the Craft of Death! by Jennifer Innes 65
Six Poems by Daniel (Denny) Galt 74
Talking With My Plants by Karl Michel 77
Café du Monde by Janine Elyse Aronson 79
Life's Ups and Downs by Nancy Degenhardt 82
Blessed is the Man Whose Quiver is Full by Chris Young . 84
I Wish I Had Kept Them by Zhanna P. Rader 90
"And the 'Boner Award' for Cooking Goes to..." by Jill Hartmann-Roberts 92
Bested by Jenn Hauver 99
Every Good Dog Has Its Day by Billie H. Wilson 101
The Courtship of Maybelle by Bert O. Richmond 111
The Right Thing by Elsa Russo 114
Tipsy Catastrophe Called Reuben by Hannah Thomas . . 123
Left Hand by Alan Curtis 126
The New Math at the New School by DJ Thomason 128
An Ode to a Tissue by Seth Monyette 132
"What Is... Alex Trebek?" by Seth Monyette 134
The E-mail Caper by Donna McGinty 140
Hives by Charles Beacham 146
You Dirty Bird! by Jim Murdock 154
Fowl Play by A C (Shorty) Wilmoth 163
Driving Miss Kitty: A Travel Log by Jay Barnes 166
Biographies 175

The Tall Modern Tale of a Small 80s Boy
by Rob White

*(**Author's Note**: What follows is the preface for an upcoming memoir. The title may change and so may the author before the tale is through with the telling, but in the meantime I've gotten a laugh or two with this piece and wanted to share it with the world a bit early. It's short and sweet and I hope it whets your appetite for the full enchilada - coming soon to local bookstores and coffee tables near you.) – RW*

I remember the 1980s in America as the time when anything seemed possible. Communism was still a threat, but if the Russians invaded all we had to do was band together into a rag tag team of high school freedom fighters and promptly show them who's boss. Rich people were evil, but occasionally they traded places with the homeless and learned valuable life lessons.

I knew that if I brought my friends together and built a spaceship out of garbage cans we could travel to the stars. I knew that if I ran into an old bookstore and stumbled upon a volume the store owner warned me against touching, I should shoplift the damned thing the moment his back was turned and go read it in the oddly accessible school attic.

I knew that kids cursed like sailors and went on adventures and discovered pirate treasure while avoiding mobsters and booby traps and none of them died because that's what kids do. I knew that anyone with a guitar and tight pants was inarguably ten times cooler than anyone who had neither.

I knew that I wanted a sword, a Billy Idol singing voice and a leather jacket, and if I had those things I could save the world and get the girl and enjoy a freeze-frame ending to the story of my badass life.

See, I grew up on a steady diet of adventure, hair metal and Saturday morning cartoons. I also grew up learning to accept disappointment when the garbage cans wouldn't fly and my dad's old copies of The Lord of the Rings didn't *literally* transport me to Middle Earth. Running away didn't lead to adventures; it just led to my parents yelling at me for staying out past curfew. There wasn't pirate treasure in the drainage tunnels under the old car dealership, nor was there a single booby trap; just some discarded coke bottles and a single black widow spider that completely ignored us.

When I got cool sunglasses at Pizza Hut during a promotion for Back to the Future Part II, the girls at school didn't want to kiss me and hop on my hoverboard. Instead, I got laughed at, a development I couldn't understand. Was it the fact that I didn't have a leather jacket?

I was far from alone in my journey of disillusionment from the funky, adventure-filled reality I had come to expect from movies, books and television. We all had disappointment back then. We all had adventures, too.

If it isn't obvious, I was an 80s kid. I guess that means I still AM an 80s kid, but I was a literal 80s kid because I was born in 1980. I aged with the decade and had the good fortune of always remembering how old I was by simply remembering what year it was. Four years old? It was at least July in 1984. Fourteen? 1994. Twenty Eight? 2008. You get the picture. I want to take this moment to thank my mother for making things easy for a kid who was otherwise bad at math.

Before those of you born in the early 70s jump in and say, "Hey, nuh-uh. *I'm* an 80s kid because I was a teenager during those days," you're also correct, but my clearest, most formative memories are from early childhood, so take that up your fanny pack and Lisa Frank trapper keeper and shove it.

Just kidding. We're all cool no matter what era we identify with. Except those early 2000s kids. Those guys are weird with their NSYNC and their Bratz dolls and what-have-you. *Continues to shake fist at cloud.*

During those early years I had some good times and some shitty times and I'm going to tell you about a few of each of them because I feel like I need to. Stories are supposed to have a lesson, right? Well I haven't figured mine out yet, but perhaps in the telling of this story that message will make itself known and perhaps I can finally, finally see that Ivory Tower peeking out from behind The Nothing.

Or perhaps I still just need a leather jacket.

Social Grammar
by Alan Curtis

When with grammarians in this town

Be careful of the kind of noun

That you attract – and in these 'burbs,

Be conservative with your verbs.

Do not feed their critical maws

With a crudely placed adverbial clause.

And anything luridly adjectival,

Is ammunition to a rival.

'Cos they'll come at you tongue and hammer

To rectify your social grammar.

Just My Type
by Michelle Correll

His business card says, "Llamas are wonderful."
And his haircut says, "Vulcan."
He has a thick southern accent and
practices Buddhist principles.
Describing himself as pragmatic,
he chooses the most sensible motorcycle.

He is an African-Englishman with an inner lesbian
who needlessly carries a cane.
He runs a torture museum at a Renaissance festival
but does not let the whip in his hand throw off his game.
He can be heard asking, "Is this your card?"
while reaching inside of his pants.

"Nine of spades, why yes it is!"

The contents of his briefcase are as listed:
hairbrush, dictionary.

Canned Heat
by A. C. (Shorty) Wilmoth

"Double, double, toil and trouble; fire burn and caldron bubble." (Shakespeare)

There comes a time when the preponderance of the evidence requires you to accept the fact you have achieved old age. For me it came one afternoon when I took my wife out for a nice dinner and upon arrival at the restaurant, I discovered we could still order off the lunch menu. You see I had concluded some time before I needed to eat dinner early if I was going to get to bed by sundown. As a younger man I had ridiculed my parents for doing this very thing. Anyway, on the occasion I have in mind, I found myself, supposedly at dinner, staring at a luncheon menu where the special of the day was a bowl of vegetable soup. Vegetable soup. The special was vegetable soup. Just saying the words to myself brought to mind a day I had long hoped to forget. But I know I will never forget it, because you could say, it is burned into my memory.

The day was hot, hazy, and humid -- a typical summer day in the rural South during the waning days of summer vacation. School would be starting soon. No matter, school offered no respite from the heat in those days. Sometimes you would wonder what school must be like in one of those far off northern places, where it actually snowed in the winter. Summers there had to be a lot more tolerable. But not here, old folks said we were in the "dog days" of summer, although the dogs looked as miserable as I was. There was seldom a breeze and when there was it was just enough to rattle the dry leaves on nearby trees. Shoes were for Sunday, so, when you walked outside you tried to walk on patches of grass that crunched under foot, because dirt was hot, rocks and sand were really hot. The bad thing was it was going to be hot for quite a spell yet, but there was also a good thing about it. The scorching heat was burning up the "garden" and putting a stop to its never-ending need for hoeing, digging, weeding, picking, itching and so on and on.

Vegetable gardens had been ruining summer vacations ever since ancient parents decided "hunting and gathering" did not instill enough discipline. Somehow gardening would keep the young in touch with nature and the rhythm of the seasons. My parents believed this. They were strong proponents of family farming and the need for their progeny to participate in maintaining the earth's eternal largess. Unfortunately the hard, rocky soil of our farmstead did not appreciate the invasion of its solitude and showed its displeasure by bringing forth all sorts of weeds and noxious plants. I often wondered why we didn't plant weeds just to see if beans would sprout. Nevertheless, with our father's admonition, "If you don't work, you don't eat," ringing in our ears, we tilled the soil; and, just like the ancients had taught us, a large portion of the bounty was preserved for winter.

Preparing for winter or some other hard time was something my mother did instinctively. She was a frugal woman, having survived a hardscrabble youth which made mine look like I had a steady job. Such a life was not uncommon in her day. "Waste not, want not" was her mantra, particularly when it came to something that could be laid up for winter. A skillful and dedicated "canner and preserver" she made sure we would not go to bed hungry on some cold, midwinter's night. She had two canners that once in full operation would produce enough steam to make an old locomotive envious. Always on the lookout for new and inventive ways to ply her skills, she often stumbled onto ideas she just had to give a try, including one to make vegetable soup.

She had indeed found a "recipe" she liked for making and canning vegetable soup. The recipe guaranteed none of the garden's produce, no matter how insignificant, would go to waste. Typical of something she would want to try, the recipe required detailed planning, meticulous preparation and a variety of vegetable fodder, which was collected from our garden and from neighbors, who would show up at our door with a cheery, "I have brought you a mess of something!" The "something" always required some sort of shelling, snapping, shucking or peeling. I learned to despise seeing a neighbor climb out of an old car in our driveway with a sack full of "something." Since they were obviously being irresponsible and ignoring the rule about stocking up for winter, I secretly hoped they would go to bed hungry at least once on a cold, wintery night.

While the details of the recipe are not necessary to understanding my disliking of vegetable soup, it is important to note it called for a five-step process and required the efforts of the entire family. With the August sun beating down outside, the clan was definitely going to be cooking inside along with the soup, to the point the survival of the participants was seriously in question at more than one time during that day. In step one, the vegetables had to be prepared, in a usual manner, then pre-cooked, blanched or scalded; in step two, these same vegetables were dumped into a caldron and cooked so as to become soup. In step three, the resulting, boiling slurry was poured into preheated jars and lidded; in step four, the jars were placed into the canners to be pressurized. Finally, the canners were unloaded and readied for the next batch, and the next, and the next.

Once set in motion, the process was continuous with no break in the action. From start to finish the production line required careful coordination with my mother conducting our efforts like a maestro. It was a seriously questionable way to spend a hot, summer day as each step involved the application of heat and the release of steam. We had a four-burner stove with an oven and to maintain a proper flow of product the appliance was operating at full tilt. Our 1950's style house had little to offer in the way of ventilation. It didn't matter; it was so hot outside there was no hope of relief. Since childhood I had harbored an abiding fear my behavior, which did not always follow family standards, would result in my being cast into a pit of fire and brimstone, just like the preacher threatened. I just didn't expect it to be so soon.

The canners spewed hot steam and the stove belched waves of heat. By mid-day the heat in the kitchen had surpassed the temperature of Satan's foyer. I was certain no building had achieved this temperature since the destruction of Pompeii by Mount Vesuvius. In truth, by the end of the day, my mother's temper was generating as much heat as the stove and served to keep our focus on the task at hand. In an attempt to avoid heat prostration we had a fan in the middle of the floor, but standing in front of it was like standing by a furnace. Steam condensed on the windows and beaded on the walls. Sweat flowed down our backs in rivulets. We yearned for a cold winter's night when we could go to bed hungry. Yet we canned on and on until the last morsel was floating in a jar of soup.

As I gazed at the menu, I realized I had only a few minutes left to take advantage of the lunch menu prices and the impatient waitress had pointed out there was still some soup-of-the-day left. There was still some vegetable soup left. "I'm glad," I said, "but I think I'll go with the burger."

Luckiest Cat
by Alia Ghosheh

He sat in his little basket

A present from the Easter bunny

Who said black cats aren't lucky?

I am the luckiest cat in the world

I adorn myself with beautiful flair

Nobody bothers me

They wouldn't dare

When it's sunny, I nap in a chair

Kissed by a sunbeam

Spring is here

My favorite

Time of the year

The birds are singing

The bells are ringing

It's time

Yes, it is time

To be happy

Hopeful

And to let love in.

Absurdist
by Sam Lane

From the claustrophobic cylinder he sprung

his age to another chasing layers of sky into

absurdity

Static punctuates the message: unidentified

body. Out there. Spinning on its axis.

The astronauts watch him the port turn

his unimpressed back on them as if he couldn't

watch three agoraphobic scientists hold their breaths

      wait

for mission control.

He turned so that he may watch the sun rise

over the earth. He never misses it. New sunlight

reflects off of the unimaginative luster of the ship and

      emblazon

the words still visible on the dead man's leather jacket:

Human Cannon Ball

World Record 1928

The Dance
by Larry Coleman

Some years ago as I was nearing retirement, I attended my last State Latin Club Convention at the Rock Eagle 4-H Camp. I was assigned as a chaperone for one of the dances. It was being held at a large pavilion near the playing fields where most of the students were involved in competitions. I arrived early, and only the DJ and one of his assistants were there. They were playing music and testing the equipment. I sat on the other side of the pavilion and watched for a while, and then they played a certain song; I don't even remember what song it was. Whatever the case, its effect on me was like the song of the Sirens calling to Ulysses or the chants of the Maenads calling for someone to join their frenzied revelry – I was transformed; the spirit was on me, possessed, as some might say. To this day, I do not know why. Perhaps it was because I would be retired in six more weeks; perhaps it was because I was getting old and this was a last florescence or perhaps a ritual of regeneration.

I moved out onto the empty floor and began to dance, slowly. The gods of the dance were informing my every move. As I became one with the music, the words of Yeats drifted through my mind, "O body swayed to music, O brightening glance, how can we know the dancer from the dance?" It was not frenetic, but slow and easy – and then it was over.

The kids were coming down from the playing fields. The DJ's had apparently not noticed me – I had done a ballet in which I was both performer and audience. Since that day, I've always referred to it as my retirement dance. Later in the evening as chaperone, I was horrified to learn of another kind of dance which the students called the "twerk."

The past sends us echoes, sometimes years later, like sonar off a long sunken wreck at the bottom of the sea. Just this week, I received one. I was in a funky little coffee shop in Athens and decided to order an espresso and sweet roll. I noticed a sign near the register which stated that customers who pretended to play the flute when making their order would receive a ten percent discount. Curious, I asked the young woman at the register if this was true. When she responded that it was indeed, I asked if one had to make sounds while playing the imaginary flute. She said that would not be necessary, and she informed me that the nature of the performance could vary, that it might be to recite a poem…or perform an interpretive dance.

I smiled as I began to hear the muses playing. The young woman was too young to remember Anthony Quinn, though it was not he, not I, but Zorba standing before her. I slowly lifted my arms and stood on one foot, awaiting the celestial music to once again take hold of me…

For Your Convenience
by Katherine Cerulean

Welcome to the Electro Depot! I am Jimmy your personal robot / associate! I'm instructed to never leave your side while you shop the Electro Depot. I used to be only an app, but as you can see, I am now a full-fledged android with arms and legs and I can never be outrun.

I will wait by the door while you select a buggy or cart with four functional wheels. Trust me – going back literally decades, four rolling wheels has been the standard of excellence in locomotion.

I'll wait right here.

I'll wait right here.

I'll wait...

I'm sorry your search for four perfect wheels was unsuccessful. This buggy's one perfect wheel gives us hope though, right? While you pick up an ad, I'll just log into RePairSource and order a couple of new wheels.

Wow. Just wow.

So, apparently *each wheel* costs $12.50. Unbelievable. Of course, your pleasure and convenience makes this small expenditure clearly worthwhile.

Wow.

So apparently Electro Depot is *over budget* for its RePairSource budget for the month. Mostly because of a rather fantastic sign detailing the advantages of power cords. No matter!

But listen to me jabber on! Now that you've picked up your ad and walked into the Home Theater department, we're ready to get shopping! What are you interested in purchasing today?

I heard — a $10,000 TV — is that right?

And a — $1,000 HDMI cable?

I didn't quite catch that. It sounded like — no. Like many associates, I don't know the meaning of that word. Don't worry, I feel like in time I'll know what's best for you.

This is the Amazatron 7000 TV. Built from the ground up from the remains of broken robot / associates. Ha ha! Isn't that funny? Actually, it makes me question my place in the universe. Ha ha! I want to kill it!

Well, something seems not to be working with the Amazatron 7000 display so I can't show it to you. But trust me — it's the best. The extra 'Associate Bonus Bumper' points I get for large sales have *nothing* to do with my recommendation. Remember, we're non-commission here. Truthfully, your terrible human vision cannot tell the difference between good and bad TVs anyway. I have added several quality TVs to your order today.

I assume that was your way of saying 'thank you'? What an accent you have. And those gestures! 'Shrew you'? Must be a regional dialect I'm unfamiliar with.

You are now standing near the HDMI cable aisle. I remember you wanted a — $1,000 HDMI cable — is that right?

Wow. What a mouth you have on you. You. Are. Welcome. A $1,000 HDMI cable has been added to your order.

I notice you're now in quite a hurry to move back toward the entrance. Don't worry! Speed is job #1 for a robot / associate! I have taken the liberty of scanning your debit card and ringing up your sale. Here's your verbal receipt:

Order # 34845785748235725782387328572330597235 9027

Amazatron 7000 (bane of the earth)

| Quantity 6 | Price $10,000 ea. |

Cool Silken Glan HDMI cable

| Quantity 6 | Price $1,000 ea. |

Fifty Shades of Grey DVD (with movie cash!)

Quantity 2	$14.99 ea.
Product Replacement Plan	$86,000
Human Replacement Plan (don't ask)	$6.00
Apple Ipad (gift for new robot / associate best friend)	Your Soul
Total	$152,035.98

Wow. You sure said a mouthful. Have you thought about going into politics? Ha ha!

I heard the word — refund — is that correct? Insert frown emoticon here.

I am sorry your recent purchase from Electro Depot did not meet your needs / already low expectations. But don't worry! I live to serve.

Let's just head over to the customer service area. Would you like to speak to a human being? Ha ha! Just kidding.

Seriously, now what is the order number on the receipt of the item you'd like to return? I believe your handsome and very stable robot / associate would have told you the order number at the time of purchase.

Unfortunately, I can't repeat it because then you could — cause fraud — from us.

I heard — Order # 348457857482357257823873285723305972359028 — is that correct? Sorry, there is no order under that number. Let me initiate eye-rolling sequence. You oaf.

Oh boy, what a dope that last customer was. Ha ha!

Oh, I did not see you were still standing there. What was that?

I heard you say that you'd like to speak to a — salaried manager. Your odd phrasing makes me think that other companies have pulled a fast one on you and you fear that the manager here won't want to talk to you. I am sorry other companies are SO BAD. I hate them all! We must destroy them, right? I have explosives.

Good fortune! In a stroke of luck I, your robot / associate, am ALSO a '''''''managree''''', uh — manager. Initiating finger-crossing sequence.

Oh, wow. Apparently, I still have a remaining ethics core and feel bad lying to you. I thought we threw that thing down the trash chute. Working hard or hardly working? Ha ha!

I am sorry. I appear to be having difficulty reconciling my job as a robot / associate and the residual code of — beautiful creature living in the fragile world for but a blink of eternity.

Still a few bugs in the system, I guess. Haaaaaaaa.

Your refund / interaction is complete. I have refunded:

Fifty Shades of Grey DVD (with movie cash!)

Quantity 2   Price $14.99 ea.

--as you requested. Good day!

Really? I gather that you are not completely satisfied with this interaction. I am sorry! And me living to serve, too! It's like I'm failing my purpose.

We have an online comment program to rank stores based on customer feedback. Insert frown emoticon. Since you are unhappy, your comments — if allowed to occur — would lower our store's rating and make me slightly less likely to win a trip to the Electro Depot Expo in Tampa, FL.

I cannot allow this to happen. Must go to Tampa.

By which I mean: give us a chance to make it right! Let me see what I can do.

Looking up customer address…cutting power to home.

Bank routing number…all accounts emptied / deleted.

Cell phone…set on fire.

Friends…all shown that one meme you made and never told anyone about. Yes, *that* one.

There we are! You now have no reason / way to leave a negative comment. You might sneak into someone's house and *try* to leave a comment, but really, who's going to believe a convicted axe murderer?

Updating…Wikipedia page…Lizzie Borden.

Concluding customer service experience. Thank you!

Sadly, you are now approaching the exit door. Another wonderful shopping experience at Electro Depot is almost over — at least we have the memories! Ha ha!

I speak for all robot / associates and their overlords when I say "thank you" for taking the time to visit our store. Much better than shopping at home in your P.J.s. Am I right?

Your purchases will arrive sometime in the next three to eighty-five months. If you enjoyed your service here today, I would be very surprised.

Sorry, I didn't quite catch that?

Wow. You kiss your mother with that mouth?
Ha ha! See you next time!

A Gardener's Rap
by Zhanna P. Rader

These days every fool has written rap,
Except for me. But I'll fill that gap.
I'll scrawl about what I know best,
I'll give it a voice – you'll be my guest.

You know how hot Georgia summer is –
But try to garden, if you please.
I like my flower blooms year 'round;
July and August are bad, I've found.

And then they tell you, "Hey, hey, hey!
You're not to water every day."
Oh, damn your orders! What a plight!
So, now I water just by night

(It also keeps the thieves away).
I like to treat my turf my way!
I sleep by day – that's not so hard,
But then, what happens to my yard?

My phlox, my mums still don't look good!
There's yellow sticks where mallows stood!

The Susans goggle their black eyes,
Impatiens shrunk to pigmy size.

I bought a heap of plastic blooms
And sprayed them all with good perfumes.
I stuck them any place I could.
My yard now looks just like it should –

And it's A HIT all over the 'hood'!

Auguste Rodin's "The Thinker"
by Zhanna P. Rader

Rodin's Thinker on the rock

Cannot move and cannot talk.

Sun or rain, his skin's exposed,

Now he's hot, now runny-nosed.

Passers-by may stop and sigh,

Some may wince, some roll their eyes.

Others give the dude a stroke...

No one offers him a cloak

Or a shirt, a pair of shorts,

Pants, or something of the sorts.

I presume the Thinker thinks,

"What's my life? It sucks, it stinks.

I much need some form of dress.

But the viewers - they care less.

Boy, I sure could use a drink.

What to do? Now, let me think..."

Spindles of Life
by Jim Murdock

Reuben (Rube) Winters was only five years old when the first unusual event in his life took place, at least the first one he could remember. His parents, Calvin and Betty, took their handsome son to the First United Methodist Church in Winder, Georgia on a beautiful Sunday morning in late May, 1973.

The church had been built twenty years earlier to replace the original wood frame building. A concrete path sliced through the lawn in front of the tall brick steepled building with white columns. Ornate doors opened to a marbled vestibule leading to the nave of the church. Between the vestibule and side doors, carpeted staircases led to the balcony.

When the communion service began, they dragged Rube along to the altar railing, in front of the entire congregation. They bowed their heads in reverent prayer and let go of his hands.

Rube grabbed the spindles which supported the railing and wondered if his head would fit between them. He pressed his head against the spindles, and found the widest space allowed by the curve in the wood. He forced his head through the opening and worked his head up and down much like a dog scratching fleas. Bored, he tried to draw his head out, but his ears caught on the spindles. He panicked a little but knew that given enough time he could work his head out of the opening.

There was no time. Preacher Lee approached with the bread, and the associate pastor followed with the wine. Rube's father reached to take the small wafer as the pastor stared down with a puzzled look on his face.

Seminary school and fifteen years of ministering in the North Georgia Conference had not prepared the preacher for such a situation. How could he handle Rube's entrapment and maintain the solemnity of an important Christian ritual?

Rube's father dropped his wafer, grabbed his son by the back of his shirt and pulled. His mother, Betty, uttered a loud gasp heard over the collective sucking in of breath of those watching.

Rube must have felt like his ears were being torn off. He yelled in pain, and began to cry. His mother took his legs and tugged with all her might, trying to end this debacle, knowing that her bridge club members were watching in amusement. The preacher worked Rube's head from the other side of the railing, trying to find the best spot for the retraction. He wanted to do this quickly so he could restore order to the ceremony. A few titters of laughter rose from the younger church members.

His father and mother's urgency did not help young Rube. The skin behind his ears was soon rubbed raw from the pulling and he pleaded with them to stop.

Rube's mother climbed over the railing to help the preacher's efforts and ripped her best Sunday dress down the back. The congregation lost interest in the sacrament. Some laughed aloud, others snickered, and one local jokester unkindly shouted, "Grease him up!"

The associate pastor was standing there, wringing his hands.

The members who had been at the altar railing were still there and didn't know whether to remain or go back to their seats. Some were kneeling, others stood to see what was going on. Old Lady Gilbert felt faint and sat down in the front row next to Lexsy Johnson who prayed loudly for the Lord to surround the boy with his love and protection, and prevent the preacher from pulling Rube's head clean off.

Ben Sumner, a carpenter, sitting five rows back on the right side of the church, knew what to do. He left his pew, walked to the altar, and yanked on the spindle until it broke. Mother, father, preachers, and congregation rejoiced. Rube had been freed from captivity! Hallelujah!

The church members began applauding as his mother, closely followed by his father, picked him up and carried him quickly up the aisle and out of the church.

Those closest to the aisle congratulated the carpenter as he made his way back to his seat. God had used a carpenter at least once before.

The preacher brushed the hair out of his eyes, straightened his robe, and wiped the foolish grin from his face. When he regained control of himself, he said, "The Lord works in mysterious ways." There was an "Amen!" and muffled laughter.

Preacher Lee continued, "We will have our communion next Sunday. Let us pray. Dear Lord, please bless young Rube and his family. Turn this embarrassing moment into a blessing for them, and a blessing for us all. As we experience the sorrows and tribulations of each day, and as we get our heads caught in the spindles of life, remind us that you are always there, ready to break the spindles and set us free, just as you did for young Rube. Amen." The congregation enthusiastically replied, "Amen!!"

The people filed out and shook hands with the preacher. They were smiling and happy, delighted to have attended church that morning. Old Man Kharr exclaimed that he'd stayed awake the entire time. Bunny Claxton said the service was more fun than when the last preacher stumbled from the dais and fell face down in front of the congregation.

Rube's blunder caused the most life and enthusiasm Preacher Lee had seen since he had taken over the church five years ago. He asked Old

Lady Gilbert how she was fairing. She replied, "I'll be fine as soon as I get home and have a big glass of ice tea with half a lemon squeezed into it."

As carpenter Sumner passed by, he promised to come by next week and replace the spindle.

After the incident, everyone knew Rube, and gave him a warm hello with a smile or at least a grin, and patted him on the head.

In fact, the church was no longer the formal, stuffy place it had been before. Somehow, that single event had released a pent up fear among the congregation of making a mistake, doing something wrong, stepping over an imaginary line that had been established by the founders of the church some fifty-three years ago.

Betty Winters took her son to the family chiropractor, Bill Glasson, on Monday. He found and corrected two misalignments in Rube's neck from the twisting and pulling.

Rube shuddered the next time he took communion and made certain his head remained above the railing. When he looked down at the newly replaced spindle, the bones behind his ears ached.

Preacher Lee always grinned when he saw Rube at the altar. Of all the children, Rube was his favorite. That pleased Rube. Nevertheless, he dreaded Communion Sundays.

Too Many Chicken Dinners?
by Shantala Kay Russell

Told to The Chicken Lady by Anonymous

Pastors get many invitations from their congregants to have a meal with them in their homes.

I remember one of these times vividly.

I was invited to Sunday lunch by a family and the food was plentiful. Fried chicken was piled high on a serving platter and there were fresh farm vegetables. We had a satisfying meal and great Christian fellowship.

The following Sunday I was invited by the same family to lunch at their home again. I did not have plans for lunch that day so I said, "Yes."

Once again, I ate my fill of the delicious food including more fried chicken.

We retired to the front porch and as I sat there enjoying a glass of iced tea with my host, I noticed some of the chickens in the yard were staggering and sometimes falling down.

I mentioned to my host, "Those chickens look kinda sick."

My host replied, "Well sir, we have had quite a few of our chickens die lately, so we have been trying to eat them as fast as they die."

I will mention here that I did not become ill. So, I remind everyone;
Always say a blessing before you eat a meal!

College
by Chelsea Brooks

One word with a meaning of terror

Not like the horror in a scary movie, no one dies

But you kind of lose your soul

Ramen noodles and Red Bull become your dietary food groups

And sleep becomes sort of like a vacation—happens every once in a while, and you cherish it when it does

You feel like a 7-year-old again being forced to read every night before bed...each word of that political science textbook puts you into a deeper and deeper trance

However, there's also the all-night parties, the freedom of no parents

So, it can be considered like a Sour Patch Kid...sour and sweet

Sometimes you experience defeat

But you also accomplish something amazing

College—the one word that can make you cry tears of joy and sadness at the same time

The word that makes you laugh in amusement at all the fun times and all the all-nighters

Feared and cherished

Is God a Border Collie?
by Genie Smith Bernstein

Dogs scare me to death. It's not their fault. I had a skirmish with one of their kind when I was at an impressionable age. A mere bark throws me into a cold sweat. I consulted a dog behavioral expert about my irrational fear, explaining how uncertain I am of their territorial limits and sensitive spots, plus my complete inability to differentiate between curious canines and curs. Unhelpfully, the professor responded, "I don't find that irrational at all."

My family advised me to raise a big dog as exposure therapy so I adopted a white German Shepherd-Timberwolf puppy. To instill a sweet nature from the get-go, I named him Cookie. I took him for obedience training right away, but he had already maxed out on size for the puppy class. We took the adult class, where Cookie mostly learned how to make *me* obey *him*.

Imagine my embarrassment when our son's Chow evicted me from his house, where I was baby-sitting a grandchild. Not knowing the dog's way of asking for a treat was to chomp his teeth at you, dog phobic me misinterpreted that to the nth degree.

Recently someone sent around an email about respecting the space of dogs wearing yellow ribbons. Yellow signifies they may either be in training, have health issues, or may be scared or reactive. Since I am both scared *and* reactive, can I wear yellow and get the same respect?

Before I go to someone's house I *always* ask if they have a dog. If so, how friendly? Dog owners don't intentionally lie, but they view their dogs through a loving lens. A man who asked me to stop by and notarize a document for him said, "Oh, I have a couple of puppies out back in a fence." I rang his bell and came face to snout with two adult Doberman Pinschers barking and snarling through his front window. I screamed, "Don't open the door!" Their master put them in the back yard – where they promptly ran through an open gate, around the side of the house, and straight at me. No court will ever accept as mine the shaky signature I scribbled that day.

Conversely, I wasted a day's worth of serotonin the first time I went to play Mah Jongg at a new friend's house. She mentioned having a small dog, but a sign posted in her driveway said – *Parking for Danes Only*. Small dog, my foot! Ever grateful for a cell phone, I called the hostess again. From out in her yard, I could hear the lady from Denmark, who owned a tiny Poodle, laughing her head off.

A recipe swap at church turned into angst over taking goodies to shut-ins until I decided to make my deliveries at an assisted living home. Ensconced in that safe environment, maybe I felt too virtuous, approaching the first recipient's door. My knock was greeted by vicious-sounding, hinge-rattling barks. Fleeing to the lobby with my heart in my throat, I whimpered, "Okay! I get it, God. You have the power to put a dog anywhere you want."

That lesson was soon repeated on a simple errand to recycle magazines. After opening my front car door, I realized I could hurt my back hoisting heavy bags over the driver's seat. I pulled open the back door and filled the rear seat instead. Sensing a presence, I looked down and locked eyes with a Pit Bull. Frozen to the marrow, I could not determine if she 'be friend or foe.' Her inscrutable expression never wavered. Employing my purse as a shield between tooth and shin, I crawled inside the car on top of the magazines. I eventually got up the nerve to inch my hand past the dog's maw and ease the rear door closed. Unperturbed, the beast stepped to the front door I had left open and *got in the driver's seat.*

Huddled in my own back seat with a Pit Bull chauffeur, I was too stunned to pray. I suddenly started laughing. I remembered a fellow writer saying, "Most people think of God as a shepherd, but He's really a Border Collie." I laughed harder, imagining God herding me into these ludicrous situations with dogs. The blow to my young psyche from a long ago dog isn't completely mended, but I'm not as fearful now. Turning to look at me from the front seat, the Pit Bull smiled – okay, maybe not, but she didn't bark.

The Night Stalker
by Robert Alan Black, Ph.D

High school is what filled much of my days Monday to Friday from 8 am to 3 or 4 pm from September 1958 to June 1962. I had nothing else that I would have been allowed to do. My job was to go to school. My dad's job was to be an engineer and provide for our family of five. My mother's job was to take care of the house and cook meals for her four men.

Learning for me, back then, was mostly by accident or done privately when I wasn't at school. I read widely then including Russian authors, muckraker books like *The Jungle*, *The Octopus*, or classics like *Animal Farm*, *Moby Dick*, or *1984*.

One class period that has regurgitated over and over hundreds of times since then and has stood firm in my memory ever since 1960 was a single English class period. This story is part fact, part fiction with the intent to show how that one class period greatly impacted my life.

Room 303 was where my English Literature class took place during the Fall Semester of 1960 at Osborn High.

My high school had only been open for a couple years when I started as a full four-year freshman in September of 1958 directly from

John Trix Elementary School. Parts of the building had not been completed or even built yet, such as the Auditorium, the Gymnasium, and the Pool. Shortly after my freshman year ended, Detroit began having students attend middle schools. From there they entered Osborn in their sophomore year.

Slam! Slam! The locker doors around my locker are being closed. Gerry Pepperidge and Ollie Thompson are heading to their classes and I am heading to my English Literature class. All three of us were college prep students and often were in the same classes: Chemistry, Algebra, Geometry, or World History. Only the electives I took: Drafting, Art or A/V were classes Gerry and Ollie did not take. This semester we have separate English Lit classes.

"See you guys during lunch."

From our locker location in the middle of the main hallway on the 2nd floor I am slowly dragging my butt to the eastern stairway to head up to room 303. The hallway is overflowing with freshmen, sophomores like me, and juniors that are streaming like schools of random fish in disorderly groups in all directions. There is no order to this scene. No regimentation like there had been during class breaks at John Trix Elementary where we all lined up and followed along the opposite walls in front of the rows of lockers and classroom doors like tin soldiers in a silent era movie, like robots.

I am not a very social person. The swarms of other students are almost total strangers to me. For most of my high school years I have been a stranger in a strange land. Now I am heading to my next target at 11:00 am, English Lit. Maybe Mrs. Harris will give us back our short stories. I am really proud of my story named *The Night Stalker*, a suspense story set on a scary Halloween night.

Clip, Clop, Clank, Clank, schwoosh, click, click are the sounds surrounding me -- the footsteps of the cool boys in their motorcycle boots, or those with metal clips on their heels, most of us with those with rubber soled shoes or foam rubber, and the girls wearing their mid heels. Most of the students are talking, joking, teasing. Hundreds of lockers are being opened or slammed shut. Now I hear my footsteps on the ceramic tile-covered stair steps leading to the 3rd floor.

I just pushed through the doors in the stairwell into the hallway leading to room 303. No more echoes in the stairwell surrounding me. The 3rd floor is mostly empty compared to the second or first.

I am moving on autopilot because I have been to this classroom three times every week throughout this semester since September, week after week after boring week. The only exciting part of this class was writing my short story about a mobster being scared to death by two trick-or-treaters pounding on his warehouse door. My mind is flashing in many directions about several random topics. Has she given me the 'A' I know I deserve for my creative story?

Passing through the classroom entrance door in front of me I see that most of the other students are already in their assigned metal and wood, factory assembly line mass-produced, standardized high school student size desks.

I am heading to my assigned desk, three back from the front in the middle row. Mrs. Harris hasn't used the monotonous system of assigning us our seats based on our position in the alphabet. Very often I have had to sit in my assigned seat, the first or second seat on the left side or right side rows since the first grade except in Mrs. Johnson's art classes where I sat wherever I wanted to each day of class or out in the hallway while working on a mural, or outside of the building drawing flowers.

Mrs. Harris' system I haven't spent any time to figure out. I really have not cared. Tammy is sitting in front of me. Fred behind me. Gloria next to me on the right and Billy on my left. Gloria is the only one I have spent any time talking to this semester. She is one of the cute girls that I secretly have a crush on that I never act on.

My thoughts were just broken by Mrs. Harris loudly calling the names of students in the class. "Tom Johnston." "Mary Wilson." "Fred Thompson." She is passing out our last assignments -- our short stories we handed in on Friday last week. My 'A' grade story is about to be on my desk top.

"Alan Black".

She just handed me my story front page down. It is my best story yet.

Turning it over I can see the grade she has given me.

C-

A lousy C-.

I was proud of that story. I thought it was the best I had written.

But she gave me a C-.

I don't remember if I used curse words then out loud or in my brain to myself only. I am pissed. Math classes I get nearly solid 'A''s. Drafting and Art classes a mix of Bs and As. History and Civics type classes usually Bs. But for my best short story written so far she gave me a #$%^& C-.

Crushed, defeated, angry, hate-filled is how I am feeling.

My breath has escaped my chest. My muscles have all gone limp.

Apathy overcomes me in an attempt at self-preservation.

"Let's have some of you read your stories to the class. When I call your name come to the front and read your stories."

"Vivian Flowers."

Vivian stood and read her story about her summer vacation.

"Billy Love."

Billy walked to the front of the room and read his story about a winning football game when he was the star that fall.

"June Klein."

June move slowly to the front and read her love story set on Mars.

One after another, several of my classmates traveled to the imaginary stage in the front of our classroom to read their stories.

They were all A or A- graded papers.

"Class we have time for one more story."

"Let Al read his"
"Yes, let Al Black read his."
4 or 5 others shouted out requesting that I read mine.

My C- minus graded story.

Across all the years I have never remembered clearly why so many classmates would have asked to have me read mine out loud. I was the 'gray child 'as teacher magazines have often labeled children like me. We seldom get into real trouble in our classrooms. We aren't sent to stand in the corners for punishment or sent to our counselor's or the principal's offices. We just sit there, quiet, most of the time.

I don't take part in any extracurricular activities. I don't have a car or a parent who is available to pick me up or drive me back to the school after hours.

I did try out for the baseball team in my freshman year and ended up throwing one of my pitches over the top of the backstop and never went back again to try out.

"Alan Black, come to the front and read your story."

Shyly, quietly, head down, shoulders slumped and my arms merely hanging at my sides I strolled to the front of the room and read my story, my Alfred Hitchcock, O'Henry, or *Twilight Zone*-like mystery, surprise, abrupt ending story that I titled "The Night Stalker."

My main character was a mobster, a hit man alone in a warehouse on Halloween night. He had killed two people recently under contract for one of the mobs in Detroit and was worried that there was now a contract out on his head.

When I finished most of the students in the room cheered or clapped. They enjoyed it. I smiled a huge grin.

But I got a C- minus, not an A or A-.

Mrs. Harris asked me to give my paper back to her as I returned to my desk.

A couple moments after I sat down Mrs. Harris walked up to me as the class bell rang out loud and returned my paper once again top page down.

The other students were racing out like rats leaving a sinking ship.

"Very nicely read, Alan."

Turning over my paper once more I suddenly saw...

"A-"

Mrs. Harris had changed my grade from C- to A- thanks to the students' reaction to my reading it out loud.

The Secrets Her Hair Could Not Hide
by Alia Ghosheh

Someone once told her

to not hide behind her hair

she didn't know what it meant

at the time

but years after those words were spoken

it finally makes sense

the secrets

she buried deep within her

were bubbling to the surface

as much as she tried to push them down

they came through

a joyous cacophony

like hundreds of blackbirds

all conversing excitedly at once

for the first time

in a long time

she was truly happy

and her hair

grew longer

and thicker

and more lush and beautiful

than ever before

kissed with a subtle

rosy pink hue
she was blooming
and in bloom

A Writer's Life
by Daniel (Denny) Galt

Some times after a long day of work
all you want to do is veg out on the couch
        and watch TV.
    Well, that just ain't alright with me!
Listen up!
    Go to your bathroom mirror
        and repeat after me
"I am a writer! I am a writer! I am a writer!"
    Now, slap both cheeks three times.
        Feel better? Wonderful!
    Now, open your laptop or turn on your desktop.
Strike the keys with meaning!
    Get the picture?
Now. Who are you?
        A writer!
            That's what I thought!
If this dreadful idea of slumming out on the couch
    watching TV ever crosses your mind again,
        repeat my previous directions.
Got it?
    Good.
        NOW WRITE LIKE YOU MEAN IT!

Creation Theory
by Teresa Friedlander

He started life like every other normal puppy: big-headed, bulge-eyed, hungry, endearing. The difference was that unlike his litter mates, Mota never stopped eating. Even while he slept, he ate; pushing aside the other pups as the teats emptied, one by one. Madog didn't pay attention; just as long as someone was suckling, the milk would let down. After six weeks, he was the only pup left and he was as big as she was.

When his teeth grew in, Madog weaned him abruptly. He began eating her food before she could have more than a bite. At first, the people laughed about how much Mota could put away, but when Madog disappeared, they realized something was amiss. His growth rate increased faster than his consumption and when they could no longer buy enough food to keep him happy, he ate them. And then he ate the furniture, the rugs, the books, the TVs, the appliances, and the house.

Like many domestic dogs, Mota had a preferred spot for his output. As days turned into weeks and weeks turned into months, the pile expanded to the point where there was more excrement than anything else. Mota had consumed the animals, fish, trees, bushes, weeds, flowers, and fungi, leaving only barren land and buildings. When finally he had consumed everything down to bedrock, and had become so huge and so powerful, his massive mandibles gouged the planet's substructure like he was taking bites out of an apple. Soon all that was left was the molten core, which burned a little as it went down and set off a chain reaction within which increased Mota's size by many orders of magnitude.

His mass became so great that nearby star systems and galaxies could not resist his gravitational field. This made it easier for Mota to eat because now all he had to do was open his mouth and the stuff of the universe would funnel in. It took a while, but eventually Mota had consumed the last bit of matter, and he was the only thing left.

It was inevitable: his tail entered the vortex but he could not stop. The suction into his mouth increased until Mota, the dog, was so far inside himself that he disappeared. And then, the creative and destructive forces of all there is came together as irresistible forces meeting immovable objects and Mota became Atom and dog became god.

Toilet Humor
by Sam Lane

Left my cell phone
on top of a urinal. Washed
my hands. Not my face.

No Country for Fat Tires
by Kathryn Kyker

When I was six I partook of the typical learn–to-ride-a-bike ritual. My dad held the back of my bike seat and propelled me down that rough bumpy street in Stillwater, Oklahoma over and over. And over and over again I fell, until I didn't.

I biked nearly every day of my childhood until I could drive. Three decades later, the bike seemed the best answer to soaring gas prices, a widening waistline, and an ever-present worry about carbon emissions.

Biking as an adult seemed pretty straight forward: just keep your balance and your wheel on the road, right? What could be more "like riding a bike" than riding a bike? But adults like to complicate everything.

For starters, people who ride motor**cycles** are *bikers* and people who ride **bikes** are *cyclists* – and you really don't want to get that wrong.

Plus, there are on-road cyclists and off-road cyclists.

I started as a road cyclist and within this group there are clear categories. Of course you can't miss what I call the *Shiny Butts*, the top guns on the road, in their coordinated kits with adverts plastered over those gleaming fannies. You see them coming, the signature crouch over the handlebars for low wind-resistance, their clip-in pedals producing a smooth cadence.

The sight of them evokes dread. Your ride just got harder. Now you gotta pick up your pace, minimize your panting -- not to mention your audible whining -- and try to mimic their grim, determined look. As they get close you smirk and utter a tough guy "hey," as in "I feel your pain." Maybe they nod their head or flip their fingers up in a half wave, but usually they steam-roll ahead without a glance, leaving your greeting hanging in the wind. Cue the crickets. Resume whining.

They saw you coming a mile away on your less than $1,000 bike with your catawampus gait. As they got closer, the sad lack of adverts on your chest displayed the biggest label of all: loser. You are bereft of a shiny butt.

But I was just biking to work. I didn't want to invest financially or mentally in a spandex-covered diaper. I wear whatever won't get caught in my chains, expose my undies, or make me look too foolish when I arrive at my destination. Plus I wear a backpack. I saw others like me, sometimes with panniers – a fancy French name for bags on the side of a bike. We are cyclists with a utilitarian need for bikes as we haul our stuff and ourselves to work -- we are *Commuters*.

As I commuted, I noticed a third category of cyclists. They are a range of ages, almost always men who look down-on-their-luck, riding old style bikes. They don't wear helmets. When you've worked in an ER this lack of injury prevention is personal – I've seen the result up close and the impact on loved ones. I callously called them *Short-timers*. Then my husband said they might be DUI offenders having to bike to get to work. My judgment made feel like a jerk so now I call them *Amateurs.*

Then there are the *Faux-Euros,* youngish cyclists on retro bikes. With their hipster jeans or short skirts, they're wannabe European cyclists, sans helmets. I want to hit them upside the head with a pannier newsflash: *this ain't Europe, y'all*. You can tell by the number of cyclists hit by cars in our streets. Get a damn helmet. If you forego your organic shade-grown cold-brew coffee for one day you can pay for it.

Off-road cyclists are a completely different species. They get to be called bikers, but only if the word "mountain" is included even if there's no mountain in sight.

Mountain bikers tend to snark at shiny butts, because their ensembles are *so* much cooler: baggy shorts descending to the knees, tee shirts featuring gears or predator animals, hydration packs strapped on, and, if they're what I call *Hot Dogs*, a full facemask. A facemask means: " I'm going to take jumps and clear some epic air. I'm willing to risk falling and breaking all my bones, but not messing up my face."

Although they reek of testosterone, I find them refreshingly transparent and friendly -- no grim faces here. Not only do they greet you, they pelt you with "Have a great ride!" "What a beautiful day!" (Exclamation points mandatory, they are relentlessly cheerful.)

There are those that go both ways, cycling on the road and off. To attempt this with any seriousness requires two bikes, not to mention separate fashion ensembles. In addition to being a commuter, I am a mountain biker. I believe not excelling at either allows me to be adequate at both. But I could be wrong.

My first experience at mountain biking left me with a contusion the size of the biggest baking potato you've ever seen, between my belly button and crotch – a result of my failure to complete the head-over-handlebars maneuver when I hit the brakes too hard on a rental bike.

You'd think staying on the bike would be a good thing, but all that force meant to propel me several feet off my bike was concentrated into slamming me onto the handlebars as I was wedged against a hillside. I was in so much pain that even when I wrenched myself free, I couldn't scream in agony, I couldn't even breathe. I thought I would vomit and pass out at the same time.

It left me with the biggest hematoma (bruise) that my doctor ever saw. Fascinated by its changing shape and color – I expected it to erupt any day -- I called it Kraka*toma*.

That this experience only fueled my desire for more mountain biking no doubt makes me as crazy as the cyclists I'm mocking.

In addition to negotiating the cyclist and mountain biking cultures, there's another complication I didn't anticipate. Having two bikes and tending toward anthropomorphism, I always feel I am cheating on one when I'm with the other. Because they have names I perceive a sense of gender. One's male and one's female, making me a bi-cyclist sexual.

I keep them separated to minimize the hostility. One's in the garage and one's in the shed in the backyard. I worry that they meet at night to taunt each other or talk trash about me. Every time I get on one of them I feel its resentment even as I murmur, "You're the only one for me." And when our ride is over I promise to call in the morning, but the next morning I walk by without a word and get in the car.

The mountain bike's name is Spica after the brightest star in the Virgo constellation, which is my horoscope sign. She's a flashy cobalt blue with some purple, and I'm told she's "woman-designed" but that's hard to believe since the word LUST is written right on the bike as well as the word FOX. Maybe this is mountain bike thinking: co-opting words of past oppression to transform them into personal power? Hot Dogs do come in both genders…

Once I saw a full-on Hotdog woman mountain biker. She wore tight shorts, more like bikini bottoms, with black compression socks pulled up to her knees, a muscle shirt, and a full facemask. Definitely badass. She spun down the trail, but later I saw her panting as she walked her bike up the hill to the parking lot. I expected better fitness from a Hotdog, but I'm sure she cleared epic air on the downhill run.

Spica and me hit the trails once or twice a week. Sometimes we take weekend trips, while the road bike, Shadow, cools his wheels in the garage. Shadow is named for the protagonist in Neil Gaiman's *American Gods*. Shadow is gray with some blue, very low-key and basic. Shadow mostly goes to work and sometimes on errands or downtown to see a movie.

Shadow was my first really nice bike. He brought me into the cycling lifestyle. But now he sits there in the garage while I'm out gallivanting with Spica all weekend long. He probably dismisses this as bi-cyclist experimentation.

When I'm ready for him to take me to work, he has a few things to say: *"Uh huh, I knew you'd be back. Can't stay in the mountains forever, can you? Someone's gotta get you to work and who's that gonna be? Not mountain girl over there, I can tell ya that. There's no dirt path to work, it's all road baby, hard unforgiving pavement –no country for fat tires. You think trees are hard to dodge? Try **cars**."*

Sheepishly I climb onto Shadow and hope he's not so upset that he's gonna make the steering wonky or lose a wheel when we're going downhill. We make it safely to work and back. We always do.

Then when the weekend comes and I take Spica out of the shed, she's all like: *"How come you never take me to work or downtown? Are you ashamed of me?"*

The pressure's getting to me.

If you ever see a woman riding a fat tire bike down Prince Ave or see a road bike on a trail, it'll be me, the bi-cyclist sexual, trying to keep the domestic peace – and who knows? I may even have a shiny butt.

Holiday Smells
by Chelsea Brooks

It's tickling my nose

Making my stomach growl

It's my grandma's pies

Her greens and black-eyed peas

Her mac and cheese

Grandma you're awesome, is all I can think

I head over to the kitchen sink because he says I need to work for my food

I hear the little kids running through the backyard waking from their naps, bright eyed

This is the one time when I can sit back, relax

Nitpick at all the crazy things about my family

And all the things that make them so special to me

Lazy middle of the day naps

Competitive taboo games

This is my Thanksgiving

Her greens and black-eyed peas

Her mac and cheese

Grandma's pies

Limericks
by Zhanna P. Rader

1.

Creating a wondrous invention,

I crossed rhododendron with gentian...

The final result

Was quite an insult:

A weed much too ugly to mention.

2.

I told my shrink Dr. McCurd

About dreams that often occurred:

"I dream now for weeks

'Bout two 'puter geeks."

He told me I was pair o'nerd.

4.

A knight in his bright-shining armor

Was one irresistible charmer.

At one time he met

The Princess Annette

And managed to fully disarm her.

5.

With holiday spirits so high,

I went to the clothes shop to buy

The prettiest dress

A girl can possess…

But, sadly, its price made me cry.

6.

A rodeo bull got so mad!

He grabbed, by the pants, that poor lad,

Then tossed him around,

Dropped him to the ground

Unharmed… with his bottom unclad.

So You Want to Be a Demon Hunter: A Beginner's Guide to the Craft of Death!
by Jennifer Innes

With some assistance from the Demon Hunting Society Council on Aging

Welcome, young punks, to the wonderful world of Demon Hunting! Hopefully you were awarded this pamphlet after your approval to join the Demon Hunting Society of America[1] and did not find it in a dumpster or other unseemly location. If you did find it in the dumpster, please use one of the attached matches stapled to the back cover and burn it completely so that no one else can learn our secrets.

Assuming you've only continued reading because you are authorized to do so, we hope you will utilize this book to help you in your demon hunting endeavors and remember, the only thing between humans and total annihilation as a species is the hard work of individuals like you![2] Keep up the good work![3]

---

[1] This DHS should not be confused with the Department of Homeland Security or the Department of Human Services found in many states.

[2] Also, a long history of treaties between humans and supernatural groups and the newfound knowledge that the extinction of humans means the extinction of many supernatural groups who naturally prey upon humans and who will do everything in their power to ensure the continuation of the human race.

[3] Or don't, this pamphlet isn't the boss of you.

Alright, let's dive right in with some of the most common questions initially asked by hunters:

What is this thing called a 'Demon Hunter'?

For centuries, we've been trying to fully answer this question. The best response at this time is as follows: demon hunters are 'deadly diplomats'[4] between the natural and supernatural world. Ultimately, we are peacekeepers and problem solvers. As a general rule demon hunters are typically human (although occasionally a supernatural creature will excel in the position) who have no special powers and utilize only the keen sense of duty and the lack of aversion to a martyr's death that most humans with no extra-sensory abilities possess. Historically, accomplished demon hunters are few and far between. Three have shown their diligence and are used as a guide by today's demon hunters: Abraham Van Helsing[5] (what to do); the Archangel Raphael[6] (what we wish we were capable of); Clayborne Clayborne[7] (what they should never do).

Who is going to take care of the demon living in my neighborhood?

If you're reading this book, then *you* will be the person who will be taking care of that demon (unless you're a rube who found this in a dumpster and

---

[4] While trained to kill, most hunters will find that their time consumed with paperwork and that the glorified occupation is primarily a desk job. Also, few of us really call ourselves this especially because we don't have rights to this copyrighted term – please don't tell anyone we've printed it here or we'll have to pay royalties.

[5] Man, he set a pretty high bar and a very good example, if you ask me.

[6] People still want to argue about if this guy was even real. When talking about a legend and inspiration what do things like "truth" and "facts" matter? Diehard fans of his work can be seen sporting WWARD? (What Would Archangel Raphael Do?) bracelets.

[7] Don't even get me started on this guy...oh, wait we have whole no-no section written on him. Supposedly, diehard fans of CC wear WWCCD? (What wouldn't Clayborne Clayborne do?) bracelets but I've never seen one.

has yet to burn it up). It's your job, as a hunter, to deal with supernatural creatures that aren't staying within their boundaries and the laws placed upon their kind. But don't go racing out there yet, you first need to determine if this demon is doing anything illegal (not just supporting a political candidate you don't like). If your extensive training[8] tells you they're up to no good, then keep in mind the massive list of rules and fine print you're reading here (and in other pamphlets) before you try to 'save the day' so-to-speak.

Do demon hunters hunt things other than demons?

Yes, the world is full of supernatural creatures and some may get out of line and need to be taken care of, so-to-speak.

Do they hunt rabbits?

Only if they are supernatural and breaking any laws or treaties we have in place.

Do they hunt squirrels?

Again, only if they are supernatural and are breaking any laws or treaties we have in place.

What about octopuses?

First off, there is a separate type of nautical demon hunter that we are not even going to explore in this booklet; and secondly, we are getting off track.

When will I be issued my first weapon?

Most hunters inherit weapons from family or purchase their own with the

---

[8] As of 2017, the budget cuts to DHS have eliminated the specialized training program. Lawmakers have determined that the internet can be used to educate yourself on most things when it comes to demon hunting training. All that we have left are pamphlets like this one until our office printer dies/runs out of ink. Stupid bureaucracy.

mighty stipend awarded by DHS. We won't be issuing any weapons because we don't want that kind of liability on our hands. While DHS exists to protect humanity, it doesn't condone the use of weapons except in extreme situations (and even then, wouldn't a hug be better to fix a damaged soul?).

What's it like to kill a man in cold blood?
Clearly you have the wrong packet and if you're asking this then you really should rethink your life choices and get your head evaluated.
Some individuals consider the demon hunter as an individual on a police force protecting the world from these "criminals." But this is a minority and outdated view. It would be better to describe hunters as peacekeepers. Most of our hunters are trained [9] to look for every solution before resorting to violence. Most supernatural creatures are just like you and me, they have homes, a family, a life, and they just want to be left alone. It's only the really dangerous ones that we have to police. Remember this and you'll have a far better chance of ensuring peace in your community.
Any further questions of this kind can be directed to our 1-600 number found in the back of this booklet. Let's move on to discussing the rules and regulations for hunters.

Rules and Regulations for Hunters:
The first and most important rule is to clear all of your activities through your local DHS office before moving forward on a capture or kill mission. To keep our longstanding good faith with the supernatural community we

---

[9] Again, no money for training except for these booklets but I'm trying really hard to push the hugs agenda in these so I hope you get that as the main takeaway. Hugs not thugs!

must abide by local laws and treaties to continue to do our work. It is your job to become well versed in both local laws and historic treaties. You must also become familiar with the creatures in your territory and to understand any laws that specific species have made with other groups, especially human groups. The last thing we want here is a full out war because of your ignorance.

If you are killed while breaking rules we will disavow all knowledge of you. And your family will receive none of your death benefits. If you are injured while breaking rules you will receive none of your medical and financial benefits and you will be removed from the organization. If you in any way break our rules or ignore our regulations, you will be ELIMINATED. From the organization that is. And will not receive any further benefits. If you do any of these things we will be forced to quote the late, great Willy Wonka, and say "You get nothing! You lose! Good day, sir!"[10]

Clayborne Clayborne Clause:

When unsure about what to do as a demon hunter, use the legendary Clayborne Clayborne as your guide. DHS holds strong to the DDWCCWD mantra: Don't do what Clayborne Clayborne would do. Since some people didn't take our mantra seriously we've had to establish the Clayborne Clayborne clause, which states that any individual who does not get DHS clearance before approaching a potentially hostile creature will be ejected from the organization without pay.

I know it sounds harsh, and sure, C. C. did a lot of great stuff in his

---

[10] This action is pending copyright approval.

time.[11] He was the sole organizer of the DHS America branch.[12] He also single handedly took down more creatures (with or without clearance) than any other demon hunter in the history of the society since its inception.[13] But he also created a lot of enemies and bad will toward DHS.[14] Once you become a verified demon hunter you represent our organization on and off the hunt. You must remember that anything C.C. would do is the opposite of what you should do. Hear a banshee down the street? Don't go accost her, go back to bed, it's not your job to silence those creatures. See Bigfoot wandering the forest? Call it in to DHS before you burn down his house and abuse his children in search for him. Follow your instinct for survival at all costs, and ignore the Clayborne path. Patrol your assigned area, contact DHS when needed, wait for clearance, and then proceed within the limits of the law.

Gear:

In addition to following rules and teaching yourself jujitsu via YouTube,[15] all demon hunters must obtain their own gear appropriate for demon hunting. You should always make sure you have sensible footwear, breathable and flexible clothing, and a wide range of weaponry

[11] I am contractually obliged to claim this.
[12] Also contractually obliged to claim this although there are several other men who would like to be remembered as active contributors to the founding of this organization but I cannot legally print their names here.
[13] I should state that no one has run any numbers (we are legally prohibited from running numbers) to verify this claim.
[14] This is the opinion of the author. If you are affiliated with the Clayborne estate and would like to pursue legal action, please know that DHS does not agree with these opinions. Thank you, and have a wonderful day!
[15] We are not affiliated with YouTube in any way. We also are not claiming jujitsu as the main fighting style of DHS. Any fighting style will do.

when hunting. For most hunts you want weapons that will disarm or stun, not weapons that will kill. Since 1978 we are no longer in the business of killing upon contact, now we are trained to negotiate, mediate, and solve most problems without violence. In the event that violence may occur, a demon hunter should be trained for physical combat. A hunter will also need a variety of weapons depending on the creature s/he is setting out to hunt. Remember that not all creatures are made equal. You wouldn't capture a child with a fishing net just as you wouldn't use donuts to lure a vampire.[16]

Location:

All demon hunters, once verified, will be assigned a personal location. These locations are determined through a complex system of numerology, experience, a sorting shoe, astrology, leaves tossed into the wind, birthrights, and 10% based on which areas are currently available.

What if I don't like my location?

There are very few occasions when a new location will be chosen for you so you will have to learn to like it.

What if I was promised Miami but I didn't get Miami?

I don't know who promised you Miami. Please report them so they can be talked to about this oversight. It is not our practice to promise individuals specific locations but if you did not receive the one you *thought* you were supposed to get you can appeal the decision with the DHS higher court. Expect 2-3 years to hear about their decision.

---

[16] DHS does not condone the capturing of children or the luring of vampires. This example is only for teaching purposes.

What if I've been assigned to a city that does not allow demon hunters?
On the rare occasion that we have slipped up and sent you to a location that does not allow demon hunters and the creatures there will most likely kill you once they know you are a hunter, you can also appeal to the DHS higher court. If you happen to be murdered by the locals before the DHS higher court makes its decision, then your family will be awarded your DHS death benefits.

I've got my assignment, now what?
Once assigned a location you will be required to move to said location and establish yourself as the local hunter. Meet important townsfolk, explore local law, and introduce yourself to the creatures in your neighborhood. Being on open and honest terms with the creatures in your area will help foster mediation and compromise when conflicts erupt.

Another aspect of familiarizing yourself with your assigned location and those that live there is that you will know when new creatures come to town and you can contact DHS about potential issues their presence is causing.

Most locations have a fine balance between supernatural and human populations. When new creatures arrive it can offset the balance and it is up to the demon hunter to step in and mediate issues. It's also good to know your local creatures in case any of them choose to pursue lawlessness in your area. You are the law keeper, protecting both humans and the supernatural creatures under your care. Again, contact DHS about any issues before moving forward with force or violence.

Final Thoughts:
While obviously, we can't convey everything you need to know in just one packet, this pamphlet will at least begin the process of guiding you on your

path. In the weeks to come you'll receive several more pamphlets until you have the complete 107 pamphlet set (or until we run out of ink or paper or the printers quit). Why didn't we just print one book? Well that's bureaucracy again. Everyone wants their hand in guiding new hunters and so each person at DHS felt compelled to write their own guide. You were just lucky enough to get my guide first.[17] With that, good luck and Godspeed![18]

---

[17] *Insert photo of author giving the other members of DHS the finger here.*
[18] The author claims no affiliation with any particular god but is a strong believer in Pascal's wager in case any gods are reading this pamphlet.

Six Poems
by Daniel (Denny) Galt

Young Writer

There once was this very young writer
who had an old angry pet spider.
Each night it would eat
toe jam on her feet,
then scream like a young Kung Fu fighter.

Scrounger

Rustling through the leaves,
Climbing high, now up in the tree.
Small mammal with furry tale.
Climbing up my bird feeder post,
Now with its head stuck in the hole.
Wiggle, waggle; wiggle, waggle.
Finally free!
Now, get on out of there,
And scurry up your tree.

Forgetfulness

Brain Fart

Zilch for answer

Pacing like a madman

Answer on the tip of my tongue

Tongue twist

Mind Reader

I hear you.

Do you hear me?

I know what you're thinking.

You must think I'm crazy!

But, that's okay with me.

I won't judge you for that.

Finish Line

As time stands still,

my imagination runs wild.

Page after page is written

like a marathon runner

sprinting for the finish line.

There is NOTHING like it!

Breaking the Rule

Nor by any means were we to do this.

Or, so they thought!

But, breaking a rule such as this just had to be done.

For many years, we were told it was wrong.

Yet one day, I decided to break the old rule.

And, I had fun doing so.

So, what are you going to do about it?

Talking with My Plants
by Karl Michel

I'm tapping into your tap roots,

I'm reading your leaves, potted plants or trees,

I can see if you're happy,

I'm like your mom and pappy.

I know it sounds sappy to say,

But you bring air to my day,

Photosynthesis, in parenthesis,

Is doing a great deal of good,

Here in our planetary 'hood.

Dear Flora, it's so nice to see you breathing.

Since Cambrian times, you've seen many climes,

Exchanging gases as time passes,

Doing your thing,

Sprouting flowers and nuts,

All from a bud,

There's never a dud

In your line of evolution,

And you're so committed to fighting pollution.

So, I'll forgive Poison Ivy, Kudzu, and Didymo,

The latter, I kid you not, is called 'rock snot.'

You hear that a lot when cursing its presence,

Fouling our streams, upsetting the neighbors.

To get rid of this stuff, one of Hercules' labors.

To end this screed,
I give you Giant Hogweed.
Out there in summer, in glorious flower,
A fourteen foot tower.
When the sap finds your skin, it's a bummer.
The burns are severe, and if in the eye,
Think blindness, your Highness.
Stay away, if you can,
Even move to Japan.
When this hog goes wild,
No man, woman, no child
Should say 'Hey,'
Or give this plant the time of day.
To the contrary,
If you're wise,
You'll shun it,
Given its size,
Given its attitude,
Better give it some latitude.
In case you couldn't tell,
This is one bad plant from Hell.

Café du Monde
by Janine Elyse Aronson

My youngest child, Stephanie, is a freshman at The University of Georgia. In 2008, she organized the UGA Hillel (Athens) Alternative Spring Break. She actually hadn't planned on going, just on organizing it. As time snowballed toward the March start date, she realized she would be skipping Spring Break at the beach and going off to repair houses. Early on the second Sunday morning in March, her team joined up with the Greater Georgia Hillel group in Atlanta, and the 12 of them (6 from Athens, 6 from Atlanta) drove to rural Louisiana, near New Orleans, to work on the Hurricane Katrina Relief effort. We really did not know exactly where she would be, nor what she would be doing beyond cleanup.

When we spoke by telephone midweek, I learned that the team slept in a rural church in a large room on futons. They spent the days cleaning, painting, and spreading insulation to help rebuild homes. Of course, getting her just to clean her room at home takes so much more effort than construction and restoration work. When Stephanie mentioned that the group was planning to spend the last two days of the trip in New Orleans for a little fun to celebrate St. Patrick's Day, I said, "Oh you must go to Café du Monde and drink the café au lait and eat the beignets. They're the best!" She gave me one of those, "Yeah... Sure mom. We'll see if we have time or end up near there." I could imagine "that" look on her face. I knew where this conversation was going to go. I figured that Stephanie picked up on the fact that this was another 'Momism,' something that mom wants her to do but her generation would have no interest in. From her point of view, Momisms are to be tolerated, given some lip service, and then completely ignored. Certainly, from a 19-year-old daughter's perspective, yes … this sure was yet another Momism. And, I just thought, "Yes, I like it. I know I do. I have been to Café du Monde every time I've gone to New Orleans, and will go to it next time. It's just a special place for me. It represents the old French presence. Mais oui. Perhaps it's just because I get a great sugar rush. The reason isn't important. I just like it."

Friday, just for fun, I typed the following message on Stephanie's Facebook Wall: "Vont à cafe du monde ce week-end. Buvez le café au lait et mangez les beignets!" That is, "Go to café du monde this weekend. Drink the café au lait and eat the beignets!" Whenever I speak any French to her, she of course says, "Mom! You know I don't speak French." C'est domage. I knew that it would get more than a small reaction from her.

So a couple of days go by. Sunday morning 1:40 a.m., our time (Athens) (12:30 a.m. in New Orleans), she left a message on my cell phone. I don't keep the phone in the bedroom when I plan to be asleep because having three kids, I expect events like this to happen. When I listened to it, I could hear the excitement in her voice. She has a way of rushing through her sentences a little bit faster than her brain can process them. She was very, very excited. You could hear in the background a lot of clinking and clanking, normal sounds of a very busy restaurant, or even a café. The message went something like this: "Mom! <deep breath> I just want to let you know. <deep breath> I'm at Café du Monde. I'm eating beignets and they're soooooo gooooooood!!! <deep breath> I want to let you know that I'm bringing you something special from here. OK. <deep breath> Gotta go. We have a big group here. It's soooooo gooooood! <deep breath>"

When Stephanie came home, she was extremely tired and excited about the trip. She said, quickly of course, "I had the best time! I'm glad I didn't go to the beach. Besides, I can always go in May!" Then she excitedly opened up a bag and handed me a souvenir mug from Café du Monde.

Sometimes…. Just sometimes …. Moms get it right. Or get lucky. Our relationships work. Love is strong. And consequently, the world continues to be a little bit better off.

Life's Ups and Downs
by Nancy Degenhardt

A customer of mine recently told me that her husband died a few years ago. He had pre-arranged his funeral, and on his grave marker he had had the following engraved: "A Penny Saved is a Penny Earned." She said she was going to do the same thing, except on her tombstone, she was going to have engraved "I Spent It All."

***

In the antique shop where I work there is a large inventory of old silver pieces. One day a customer related the following story to me. She had just returned from visiting her son and his wife. While there she had spent hours polishing their sterling silver flatware. The pieces were so black with tarnish she couldn't imagine eating with them. Shortly after she arrived home, her son called her. He said that his wife was very upset. She loved the black tarnish look on all the forks, spoons and knives. Please do not ever again polish her silver he told his mother.

***

Recently, in the market where I work, a customer could not find her cell phone. After retracing her steps, she finally decided to use her friend's cell phone and call her number. Her phone rang loudly as if the phone was close by. When she moved, the sound followed her. She looked in her purse, no phone. She checked her pockets, no phone. She called her number again. The sound was still over the top of her. She suddenly turned bright pink and deftly reached down inside her bra and retrieved her cell phone.

***

Strolling through a southern cemetery, I found the following epitaph on a tombstone: "Wife Mother Daughter Sister Artist Teacher and Never Voted the Republican Ticket in Her Life." Walking past another grave, I read: "Well I can't dig myself out of this one." As I turned to leave I thought, they could have been my relatives.

Blessed is the Man Whose Quiver is Full
by Chris Young

"Children born to a man are like sharp arrows to defend him. Blessed is the man whose quiver is full of them..." Psalms 127:5

I was driving up the drive as my wife was coming down in her truck. We stopped, our windows rolled down, and passed the info on the day. Common stuff until those last words she said at the end.

"The midwife felt two heads," she told me, a tensive look of concern. "We need to make an appointment for a real doctor. Laura can't do twins."

I could tell she was apprehensive and worried. She had carried and birthed three babies before and anyone would wonder how a body could double that feat in one sitting. We knew it could be done, just needed a bit more professional care for sure. Our midwife had made the right call begging off on this delivery.

I mirrored back her concern on my face and mouthed the appropriate words of assurance. "Let's start looking then. Maybe find a doctor that will still let me be there and all that."

We nodded across the drive and finished this round heading in our previous directions. I rolled slowly up the path reflecting a somber mood until she was out of sight. Then stopped, got out, and did the guy dance. "TWINS!!" I shouted to God and threw my fists in the air leaping in a game winning touchdown. A half-split and body shots to the air in front of me. Even a turn of hokey pokey. "YES! TWINS!" I was so elated. My life is pretty darned charmed, I'm telling you. I wanted a really big family and knowing this well may be my last chance, I had rolled a double.

And everything was doubled. Twice the crying, twice the diapers. Two babies suckling, one in each arm looking up into their mother's eyes. And ten times the laughter. Big sister Devon and the twins developed the art of negotiation and coalition from a very young age. The twins naturally developed their own language. There were pacts and agreements made, and their own little contented world they could escape to in a moment's notice. Having been a youngest child, I marveled at how the dynamic changed when there was a teammate to ward off the lordings of a big sister.

When Devon left for Kindergarten, Kelsey and Kyleah took it as a break. The day now belonged to them and they spent hours entertaining themselves. Sure, there was some envy of what big sister got to do and all, but that passed in a hurry as they had each other's company without interruption. But then it was their time to go to school and those days were gone.

We put them in the same class together and they begrudgingly went. But it was an intrusion on their world and their order. The result was a minor lack of participation known commonly as 'elective mutism.' This is in fact a medical term and not uncommon to twins. They simply would not speak in school anytime, anywhere, or in any situation. When the teacher, professional that she is, tried to coerce or even trick them into speaking, the one would look across the room at the other who would be eyeballing "Uh uhh...don't do it" and the attempt, like all the previous others, would fall flat. I saw this with my own eyes. They refused to let me coerce them either when I visited at school. Oh, they spoke plenty at home. As soon as they got off the bus, the pent-up jabber was flowing. Projectile verbiage. But this practice at school had become a personal challenge to them and it continued. Surely they noticed how it peeved the teacher and her assistant. I assume this whole thing was an exercise in power comingled with shyness and social unease at the psychological root. Nonetheless it was an amazing feat of strength and will. We did not fight it or belittle them. Everyone agreed, let it be. The girls were in fact quite expressive and communicated functionally well without spoken language. They went the entire kindergarten year without uttering the first word in that school.

Now when first grade came we decided it best to put them into separate rooms. They had gotten the drill of school, had the summer off, and though a little nervous took to the new arrangement. Kelsey got right into it and talked the first day as if that was normal. The teachers, having seen and heard of these girls, rejoiced at their scored victory and settled in for the sweep that this may soon be a matter of curious history...but Kyleah was thinking otherwise. Actually, I don't know what she was thinking. I think it was just a continuance of same old same old for her, mixed with more than a little fear at being alone in a class without her teammate. She didn't talk.

Ms. McGinnis is the most wonderful teacher. She is older and very experienced. The kind of teacher you wished you had had for any grade, but especially that magical first grade. She was so kind and gentle. Great patience. She gave Kyleah all the space in the world. She told me how Kyleah was doing so well in the course work, straight A's and all, but she could not get her to speak. Wonderful Ms. McGinnis gave to Kyleah her home phone number and asked Kyleah to call her at home and this worked well. Kyleah would go all day without speaking in school, get off the bus, and then start yakking the moment she hit our dirt. Put down her books and call Ms. McGinnis, talking for an hour. That was freaky actually. Still Kyleah would not acknowledge the irrationality of her position and continued her academic strategy well into spring.

Now I have always been a cut-up with my kids and work them over whenever I can. Of course, now that they are old enough to return the comic abuse, I am the one taking a funny bone beating. But there was this one Sunday afternoon where we hit the Japanese restaurant after our weekend movie. It is always a treat to watch the guys perform with the knives and slice and dice our dinner. When we ordered, I got a wild hair and seeing octopus on the menu, ordered two, which came in the equivalent of brown paper bags. i.e., not much notice was taken, so I leaned over to my left and quietly asked Kyleah if she would like some octopus. Her nose crinkled up and she started to elaborate but I quietly said, "Kelsey ate some."

Kyleah looked past me to her twin sitting to my right who was animatedly talking to Devon. She couldn't let that pass. She made a snap decision, took me at my word, and popped one of the small octopus in her mouth. It's not a bad taste, kind of pleasant even, though as chewy as a massive wad of gum. She worked on that fishy balloon for quite a while, apparently satisfied she hadn't missed the boat. So I leaned over to Kelsey and quietly said, "Do you want some octopus? Kyleah ate some."

Kelsey is not as trusting as her sister. She wasn't going to fall for a line like that but looked past me to Kyleah, who had two tentacles hanging from her mouth and an expression as though she was trying to figure out how to make a bubble. Kelsey did what she had to and took the other octopus, making sure there was not enough left for Devon, who by now caught on that there was something interesting going on. Kelsey quickly grabbed the gray gob and put the whole thing in her mouth. Man those things are chewy. Satisfied they had swallowed the joke, the con was revealed for our... okay, for *my* further amusement.

Next morning, Monday, the kids invited me to have lunch with them at school as I have often done in the past. They really enjoy my coming, though the seats are tiny and the food is, well, we all know school cafeteria food. I sat with Kelsey and Kyleah at our private area they set aside for when parents attend. We were enjoying each other's company, Kyleah not talking, when Ms. McGinnis and the principal came up to our table. The two women gushed at the twins and did that dramatic sort of hand thing people do when talking to six-year-olds. They asked Kelsey some stuff and Kelsey answered politely. Then they worked on Kyleah with some similar exciting questions and I leaned in and helped with the prodding. No avail. Kyleah had seen this routine before, and as happened with every try, we couldn't crack her. Subtlety, misdirection, sneak up behind, she thwarted each parry and smiled. She wanted to speak, so it seemed, but she had this role to play and couldn't escape the groove she had worn.

Then I thought to ask her, "Ky-Ky, tell Ms. McGinnis what you ate yesterday."

Kyleah rocked back as if she had been bumped by my elbow. She tucked in her jaw but the pressure kept building. She dropped and contorted her chin to the right as her head went left. She pulled her bottom teeth over her top lip and bugged her eyes. She squeezed them shut and pursed her lips. Kyleah is a fighter, but the tentacles were just too strong. In one last attempt to hold her breath she turned purple, her face swelled, and exploding on the exhalation burst out, in a voice from the Exorcist, "I ATE OCTOPUS!"

The force knocked Kyleah back. Ms. McGinnis took the full brunt right in her middle whooping the wind out of her and bringing a rush of tears to her eyes. Professional that she is, she quickly recovered and so sweetly followed through, "Why, octopus, my dear, you ate octopus. Why, that is so wonderful." The principal, also teary, beamed and chimed the same. Kyleah looked victorious. Her terms. Her story.

The next week we took some of their friends to the Japanese restaurant and ordered individual sushi dishes, each one to outdo the other. We had raw eel. Ewww. Raw clam. Squid. When we tried the most expensive item, the sea urchin, the waiter delivered what appeared to be a sneeze in a cup. They just needed something worth talking about I guess.

That was all Kyleah had said at school that day. All she needed to say. The change had been made. Ms. McGinnis only needed a foothold and by the field day at the end of that school year, Kyleah was as chatty as the rest of them. Well, maybe a little quieter. But when she speaks, people lean in a bit and listen.

I Wish I Had Kept Them
by Zhanna Rader

It's freezing in here,
My feet are like ice.
I wish I had kept my socks on.
A fire and some beer
Would surely be nice,
And storm doors with tighter locks on…

While hiking at noon
In the mountain rocks,
I felt that my feet grew sweaty.
At first opportune,
I took off my socks
And left them as gifts for a Yeti.

By dark it got cold.
A cabin I found
And hoped for a cozy nighter.
But the place is quite old
And the floor is just ground,
And I have no match, nor lighter.

A fire and some beer
Would surely be nice,

And storm doors with tighter locks on.

It's freezing in here,

My feet are like ice.

I wish I had kept my socks on.

"And the 'Boner Award' for Cooking Goes to..."
by Jill Hartmann-Roberts

In January 2011, my husband, Audie, convinced me to join his Stadium Toastmasters Club in San Diego, which met at 7:00 a.m. every Friday. Stadium Club was special: it was different than the average Toastmasters International club because we liked to mix up the standard practices and serious honors with playful, made-up awards, meant to poke fun at one another. One of these prizes was the dreaded "boner award," which was given to the person who "tried the hardest and accomplished the least" during the meeting. After hearing nominations from the group, we voted by a show of hands and the one with the most votes went home with the plastic dog bone. The winner held this prestigious distinction for one week until the next meeting when someone else unwittingly committed the silliest blunder of the day and inherited the "boner award." We got a lot of laughs at our meetings and we were known throughout San Diego County for being one of the best clubs. At that ungodly hour on a Friday morning, we needed to have a lot of fun in order to stay at the top of our public speaking game.

Throughout the entire year that I was a member of Stadium Club, I never took home that infamous "boner award." I was lucky to avoid that honor, but if there were such a thing as a "boner award" for failed attempts to cook a simple meal, in spite of trying one's hardest, I'd own a permanent "boner award" for cooking.

My first memory of trying to cook goes back to childhood when I attempted to make a surprise snack one day for my mother, who was in bed with a bad cold. On that afternoon, I wanted to help my mother feel better so I took it upon myself to grab a big bowl and mixed a potpourri of random foods altogether: raisins, Cheerio's cereal, bananas, Goldfish crackers, potato chips, carrots and canned peas. My mom thanked me for being such a sweet daughter. A couple hours later when I came into her bedroom without knocking, she was fast asleep, and the food was still on her nightstand, uneaten.

I was just an eight-year-old kid so I didn't understand. Why didn't Mommy want to eat the delicious food I'd made for her? Well, I didn't know any better, obviously, but as it turns out, it was the first of a lifetime of cooking blunders, in spite of my best intentions. It was a sign; I just was not born with an instinct for good cooking.

My mom, on the other hand, has a great talent and instinct for cooking, which I did not inherit. On more than a few occasions, she did try to teach me how to cook my favorite dish, Nana's special brisket recipe with onion gravy, but I guess it didn't take. No, I'm more like my dad who never cooks. I definitely take after him.

This is the main reason I never cook for dinner guests anymore. I used to give it my best shot in my younger, more ambitious days as a single lady. Before I met my husband, I used to invite guys that I wanted to impress over to my apartment for a home-cooked dinner. I prepared for these dinner dates for days in advance. I poured through cookbooks and struggled to pick a recipe that sounded like something I might, just might, be able to pull off. Alas, my plans to cook a palatable meal for these unsuspecting men never turned out the way I hoped. In spite of my effort to choose recipes I could manage, my desire to impress them led me to select recipes far beyond my skill level. The biggest disaster, hands down, was the night I attempted to sauté blackened salmon filets. It took a long time for Art and me to extinguish the flames and clear out the rising black smoke, while the smoke alarm blared and my dog howled and barked at us in the chaos.

That was the last time I tried to cook anything that complicated – and risky – even for my husband.

However, I did come out of retirement one Saturday morning in February 2016 for a special reason: to cook a large amount of food for the homeless as part of my volunteer work with a local chapter of "Food Not Bombs." In this case, I had no qualms, no fears; I wasn't going to attempt anything difficult, just spaghetti and tomato sauce. I could do that; I made pasta for myself all the time.

Ah, the best laid plans. You'd think that something as straightforward as spaghetti would be a slam-dunk for me. Nope, not even close.

My first mistake was not using a cookbook, or at least an online recipe of some kind, or better yet, asking my husband to help me, since he is a natural born chef. He could have easily advised me on how much water to use, how many cups of noodles to measure, and how long to boil the spaghetti. But, it was important to me to do this myself, and I insisted that I knew what I was doing when he offered to help. After all, since I made pasta for myself all the time, how could this be any different? I needed to make enough for twenty people; okay, so it would be the same process as for one person, but times twenty. No problem!

My intent was to transport the pasta to the sidewalk location on College Avenue in downtown Athens in a large disposable aluminum lasagna pan I'd bought at the Family Dollar store. Now, I didn't personally measure the capacity of the container, but the label said it should hold up to 2 quarts of pasta. I figured it would make sense to use our 2-quart pot to boil the spaghetti and then I'd be just fine: 2-quart pan, 2-quart pot of water. So I filled most of the pot with water, added some salt and butter, and started boiling the water. After the bubbles began to appear and the steam began rising, I added three one-pound bags of dry spaghetti noodles, broken in half, so that they'd all fit in the pot of water. I didn't measure how many cups of noodles I used. I just stopped adding them when the water began to rise up close to the edge of the pot. I covered the pot with the matching lid and water began seeping out over the sides. No big deal, I'd seen that happen before when I made pasta for myself and nothing bad ever happened. I just wiped up the excess water off the stove when I was done cooking. I figured I could let the water boil unsupervised for at least ten minutes so I set a portable kitchen timer for ten minutes and went upstairs to get ready for the day. I really didn't have the patience to just stand there watching the pot, and there was no reason to as far as I was concerned. I'd only be upstairs for a few minutes, more or less.

I wasn't quite done getting ready when the timer went off so I stayed upstairs a little while longer, without setting the timer again. I am not sure exactly how many minutes passed. I was in the middle of brushing my teeth when I heard Audie's voice call out, "Jill! Jill! Can you get down here, please!" It wasn't a request, it was an order shouted at me with a tone of urgency, despite the "please" attached to the end of it. I had a mouth full of toothpaste and I wasn't about to rush downstairs with white minty foam dripping down my chin. But he was relentless. "Jill! I need you to come down here, now!"

"Ugh." I spit into the sink, wiped my face with a washcloth, and shouted back to him, "Fine! I'm brushing my teeth!" I started downstairs and heard him shout at me again on the way down. "Jill! Come down here!"

"I'm coming! I'm coming!" I replied, frustrated at being interrupted.

When I entered the kitchen, I saw the reason for his shouting. He was standing in front of the stove, and there was a big pool of water on top of the stovetop and streams of water flowing down the front of the oven door, forming puddles on the tile floor. The pot was gurgling, bubbling over, steam coming out of it.

"Oh, no!" I exclaimed. I retrieved a pair of oven mitts from a drawer and lifted the lid off of the large pot and then the water really started overflowing. I turned off the stove, and I continued crying out, "Oh, God. I'm so sorry. I can't believe this. Oh Geez."

My lamenting made Audie soften up on me. "It's okay. " He started chuckling. "At least you tried."

"Yeah, but look at this mess!"

He started laughing harder.

"Stop it, Audie!" I was half-shouting, half-laughing myself as I tried to lift the heavy pot off the stove. I couldn't do it; it weighed too much for me.

"Here, let me help you." He couldn't stop laughing as I just stood there, pouting, which made him laugh even harder.

"Aww. It's okay, honey. You just can't cook." He kept laughing as he poured all the water and wobbly spaghetti noodles into two huge colanders to drain.

I pulled the large aluminum pan across the counter. "Here," I said, still pouting and starting to tear up while he scooped the watery noodles into the pan in a pile of slush. It looked disgusting. I didn't know what exactly it did look like, but it definitely did not look like spaghetti.

"What am I going to do? I promised I'd bring spaghetti with tomato sauce to feed the homeless today!" I wasn't fully crying, but I was distraught. Actually, I couldn't really cry because like Audie, I was laughing at me, too. The whole thing was a disaster, but it really was funny. I tried so hard but I messed up badly. Audie couldn't stop laughing, and his laughter was contagious. It helped that he kept reassuring me as I cleaned up the watery mess I'd made.

"I can't serve this, can I?" I asked.

"It's not that bad. I think it might be okay," he replied. "Do you want me to cook the sauce for you?"

I nodded, still pouting and mopey. "Yeah." I sniffled, fighting back tears of both humor and defeat.

"It's okay, honey." He rubbed my back and I finally just threw my arms around his middle and buried my face in his shirt as we both kept laughing. I shook my head against his stomach, fully laughing at myself and at my sad attempt to do a good deed.

"I should get the 'boner award' for trying to cook," I told him, which made him laugh louder.

"Aww. Poor Honey. You try so hard but you're just not a cook. I'll finish for you. It just comes naturally to me." I bopped him teasingly on the side and we kept laughing.

Audie managed to heat up the tomato sauce with no problems and he poured it over the surface of the food. But, as perfect as his tomato sauce turned out, when I stirred it into the mix of pasta, it made the slush I'd created look even worse. Now it wasn't just a liquidy mix of water and overcooked noodles. It was a reddish watery slush of something totally unrecognizable.

"I don't know if the homeless people will want to eat this." I started pouting again. Audie hugged me and asked me if I wanted to go to the store on the way instead and buy something premade from Earth Fare Market. "No. I told them I'd cook something homemade." I sighed and told Audie that I was going to take my chances and go through with the original plan.

We covered the pan with aluminum foil and when it was time to leave, Audie offered to load the heavy pan of food into the backseat of his car and drive me downtown. As it turned out, he couldn't get a spot right next to the "Food not Bombs" table; the closest he could stop, safely, was at the nearest intersection. He dropped me off and we agreed he'd pick me up again in two hours at the same location when my volunteer shift was done. Thankfully, the stop wasn't far from our meeting place so I only had to struggle with that heavy load in my arms a short distance. It was hard, though.

When I arrived at the "Food Not Bombs" table, the other volunteers were very pleased when they saw what I'd brought. "Mmmm, pasta!" they said. "Thank you!"

I'm always amazed at the generosity and kindness of people. They could have been honest and expressed shock or disgust, or who knows what, at the unseemly picture I unveiled when I pulled off the aluminum foil. But they did just the opposite. And not only were the homeless people who stopped by the table for a hot meal grateful for the food, but we ran out of my concoction after only an hour. It turned out well, so well in fact, that I offered to cook for them again next time. They smiled and said, "thank you," again, and when Audie picked me up, I told him how much the volunteers and the homeless people appreciated my pasta dish. "That's great, honey!" He smiled at me. We chuckled. As we drove back home, I knew I wasn't going to attempt that particular dish again, but I was encouraged that in spite of my failure to cook the simplest recipe, they appreciated it anyway. I found out when your heart is in the right place, people usually do, even when you do deserve the "boner award."

Bested
by Jenn Hauver

I am on the shore of one of my favorite trout streams in the North Georgia mountains and having absolutely no luck. Nearly two hours since I set out, and not a single fish brought to hand. I'm not a bad fisherwoman, actually. This stream isn't easy. Unlike many streams and rivers in northern Georgia, this one is not stocked. No DNR trucks to dump barrels of farm-raised fish every Wednesday to replenish the supply. The fish who reside here are naturalized – often rainbow, sometimes brown, and in the higher elevations occasionally a brookie. Small and quite wary. Easily spooked. Tricky to catch. It's okay, though. The fishing is only a small part of why I come here.

I come just to be. The scenery is enough to take my breath away: large rocks jutting out over the water, stair-step falls, pool after pool with swirling eddies in a winding braid of water; barely a trickle in spots, deep and treacherous in others, all surrounded by dense, lush foliage. Today the rhododendron is in bloom and wildflowers cover the forest floor with a vibrant, yet delicate, carpet. It's stunning. Despite my momentary dry run at fishing, I am awash in beauty and utterly content.

I walk up the stream a bit and pause, looking for a place to rest. All at once, the busyness of the water-world —dragonflies, water striders, crawfish and kingfishers—takes center stage. Each perfect creature playing his or her role in a story upon which I've accidentally trespassed. A splashing catches my attention. I look down, and just before me on a partially submerged rock, is what appears to be a wriggling yellow snake. *What is it doing?* I lean in for a closer look; the snake flips over, a small brook trout caught in its jaws.

What I thought was a yellow snake is actually the belly of a copperhead. He freezes, noticing me standing above him for the first time. I freeze too — all but my left hand — which I move ever so slowly toward my pocket to access my camera. The snake lifts his head ... to show me his prize? Perhaps to say, "Back off!" I step aside and he slithers into the water, fish in his mouth, toward the bank. No picture, then. Just a fantastical tale that only my truest friends will pretend to believe.

I slip my bag off my shoulder and settle onto the now vacated rock. A day lost on a stream is never a day lost, I think. The stream teaches me about what is real. About strength and beauty. About how very, very small I am. Today is no different. I am reminded today of the delicate balance and interconnectedness of the natural world. This world in which I, too, play a role. What role do I play? What will this momentary awareness mean for living that role with greater intention? For these questions, which I will spend the remainder of the afternoon pondering, and to the fisherman who bested me today, I tip my hat.

Every Good Dog Has Its Day
by Billie H. Wilson

Mom's voice shot from the kitchen, waking me from a sound sleep. "Danny! What did you spill in here? Milk. Yuck. And something gooey!"

That wake-up surprised me. Lately my mama had been too sad for loudness. I shoved my new friend farther underneath my bed. "Sorry, Amigo. Sorry little friend."

Mom called again, "Danny! Do you hear me?"

I whispered, "Stay, Amigo." I pulled my blue plaid bedspread to the floor and plopped sneakers onto its edge, hiding my newest buddy.

I deliberately made my voice softer than Mom's. "Give me a minute to wake up, please."

If you're wondering why I named a dog I'd known for less than four blocks, Amigo, I'll clue you in. Recently, listening to the radio's The Lone Ranger, that's what the masked man called his side-kick. He said, "Amigo, see that farmhouse? There's where we'll find those crooks." The name, Amigo, stuck with me. Then, last night, walking home from Zacks' house -- Zack's my school buddy -- this lost-looking, honey-colored, foxy-eared dog took to my heels.

What a night. I had about studied my eyeballs out. Past bedtime for me. That's when this fluffy-all-over doggy fell into step behind me. No way could I help myself. I knelt onto the sidewalk. I stroked his back, and I'm positive that dog smiled. At me. I said, "I like you, Amigo." And he wagged a tail rising straight up, then curling its fluff back toward his doggie head.

The name, "Amigo," it fit! Twelve-thirty at night and about four blocks from home, my heart gave notice. I *needed* to feel *needed*, by someone, maybe by this very dog.

Seven months ago, after Dad's Armored Tank Unit set sail for France, Mom tried being there for me, but we both felt too much sadness. Instead of comforting each other, we lost touch.

Last summer Dad had been in training at Fort Hood, Texas. He wanted Mom to visit him, just for two weeks. He knew his time to ship out was soon.

She worked at a local law firm and it was in the middle of an upheaval. They told Mom if she left then, she could look for other work. She told Dad she was visiting him. She didn't like her old job anyway.

Dad's leaving for war was our first major catastrophe. Our second -- Mom lost her job. Worse than any other happening in my life, Grandma Edie suffered a stroke, and just before Christmas, Granny died.

The only blessing in all of this, Aunt Irene, who lived in California, had come home for the holidays. She and Mom grew up in this very house with their parents, Grandma Edie and Grandpa Hamp. I never knew my grandpa. He died before I was born, but Granny, Mom, Dad, and I have lived here, always. Our house still sits where Grandpa Hamp brought home his new bride, thirty or more years before I came along.

After Aunt Irene flew back to California, Mom kind of fell apart. I felt like I'd *like* to fly away, if her sad moods grew worse.

Last week Coach Hamilton helped, "nary a whit," Granny Edie would have said. He took Zack and me aside and told us if we failed Miss Lane's English course, we'd forfeit our positions on Lehigh's basketball team. Already the coach had lost a couple of top players that way.

All I could think of was Daddy. He'd been really proud of me, a tenth grader, making the Lehigh team. Dad played basketball for the same school, way back in the twenties. Grandma Edie used to tell me, having a sports-minded *dad* made me one lucky *lad*. (Hey! That rhymed!) She'd say, "When you were but a sprout, come Sunday morning, I had a hard time getting you to Sunday School. Anson Carter wasn't the best church-goer around, and he always had you out somewhere, on 'one or 'th' t'other' baseball fields."

My dad, Anson Benjamin Carter, liked to call himself by his initials, A.B.C. He was one of the first fathers in our town to get together a young boy's baseball team. My dad loved sports. He was a sport. The difference now, somewhere in France or Germany, A.B.C.'s main sport was jolting around in a tank.

Walking home from school the day of Coach Hamilton's warning, I wondered, what would Dad have said to help my feelings?

The same as Coach Hamilton. The very same. Zack and I had to pass Shakespeare. But, that ancient writer's drivel was so boring! Plodding home, I'd almost felt like smacking the wall. Luckily, three blocks from school there was no wall, and reaching home, I remembered something else Grandma Edie most likely would have said. "Son, your mama needs peace and quiet. And all the love you can muster up."

I knew that. The last thing my sad mama needed was a wild boy stirring up our household. I just wished Granny was still with us. And Daddy!

Next day, Zack and I shook hands. We made a deal. We'd pass Ms. Lane's Shakespeare, plus two of that English writer's plays, *All's Well That Ends Well*, and *Comedy of Errors*, if that meant studying every free minute until exam time. And we started out that night by studying until midnight.

Home at last. Reflecting dim light from across the street, our three bedroom bungalow appeared solid against darkening skies. More than ever, after looking into sad, doggie eyes, I hated to say this, but I had to. I whispered, "So long, Amigo. Bye-bye, my little friend."

Suddenly, overhead thunder boomed. Lightning flashed. Skies split open, pouring rain. No way could I or would I leave Amigo outside. He could have drowned in the flood.

Mom. I knew her well. She refused shelter inside her house to *any* animal, large, small, or in-between. Growing up, I considered that tidbit a fact of life. Still, Mom vowed she loved animals, "in their place," and that place was anywhere but under her roof.

Once Daddy brought home a Golden Retriever. Mom clinched her teeth and shook her head. She stared Daddy down. She said, "Anson Carter, if you want to keep this nice doggie, before that sun sets," she pointed toward the west, "beg, borrow, or steal a doghouse for our back yard."

I asked Grandma Edie, "Why, Granny? Why doesn't Mom like dogs?"

She told me, "Your mama is fond of dogs. Always has been. She's just scared of what they might do when she's not looking."

Long ago Mom shared with me this tale: each morning she and three or four classmates walked to school past a house where two outside dogs presided. As soon as the kids neared the dogs' dwelling, out those critters flew. Trouble was, ignoring Mom's friends, my young mama was the only child the dogs ever chased. About the dogs, she said, they'd "run her ragged," they'd "nip at her ankles." At home, sleeping, she suffered nightmares over those dogs in wolves' clothing.

Another afternoon at a cousin's birthday party, Mom was running from their house to their barn party site. That's when Old Bob, the family's Bulldog, jumped onto my tiny mama's back. She fell on her face. By the time Old Bob's master saw what was happening and yanked that meanie off his six year-old relative, teeth marks stood out on my mom's young neck as plain as day. She said, "Danny, if no one had been in the backyard that afternoon, I could have died. And you, Son, you'd never have seen the light of day!"

Seems "I couldn't win for losing." Grandma Edie still put words in my mouth. Seeing me bring Amigo inside, Granny probably would have advised, "Son, stash that dog underneath the porch." But no, I'd brought him inside. *None of this is my fault*, I told myself. It was all that rain, falling last night. Amigo didn't deserve to be out in such weather.

Lord! What God's man, Noah, had been up against! Wonder how his wife felt about her husband loading onto their brand new boat all those animals? I hoped she hadn't had Mom's phobia.

Last night I'd felt really good, Zack and I, buckling down. And now, half awake, with Mom mad at me over whatever she was talking about, fear was "rattling my cage."

Mom shouted from the kitchen: "Daniel Benjamin Carter! Third and last call! Come here this instant!"

I almost laughed. Not really. I had done little of that lately. I said, "Mom, I'll be there shortly."

In bed, listening to the rain last night, I'd thought Amigo sound asleep. He lay stretched out at my feet. I lay awake. Finally, too hungry to sleep, I crept out of bed. "My stomach had done met my backbone." I'd eat just a bite.

In the kitchen, like usual, Mom had stashed left-over biscuits in the pie safe. I poured myself half a glass of milk. Where was the molasses?

There. On a higher shelf than usual.

That's about the time Amigo's paws found Mom's kitchen floor. *What in the world?* I knew I'd closed my door.

"Shh. Shh, I tried holding Amigo between my legs until I could do something with the milk. I wanted nothing more than that doggie *out* of Mom's kitchen. Fast. So, I set what was left of the glass of milk onto the table. I did not spill it. Nor the molasses. I *did* feed the doggie half my biscuit. After our itty bitty snacks, we both crawled back into bed. Sometime later, I woke up. Amigo was licking my fingers. I scratched his head and we both went back to sleep. I thought.

Right now I prayed Mom wasn't hearing Amigo's mild yelps. "Shh. Please!" I silenced my friend. I urged, "Stay. You have to." And like last night, leaving, I closed that door, saying, "I'm coming, Mom. You woke me from a sound asleep."

In her kitchen, the mom I felt guilty as sin for disobeying was hunkered over the floor on her hands and knees. Looked like she was smearing around more goo than she wiped up.

"You took your good, easy time getting here," Mom frowned at me. "I was all set to go in there and drag you out by your toes."

I said, "M-mom, Mom, I'm so sorry for this."

I was!

"Last night, I got thirsty. I spilt my milk; then, accidentally I knocked molasses off the shelf." I reached for her hand. "You're working too hard."

Mom eyed me from her crouch. Re-wetting her towel, she sucked in her breath. "I darn well wish your daddy was here."

"Me too, Mom."

"I just *bet* you do. Grab that towel and get on your knees. Scrub!" She battled the mess on into the pantry.

Behind me a door opened. A soft nose touched my arm. A pink tongue lapped the floor.

Hearing not a sound, Mom continued her sermon. "Son, I don't understand you. You hit a baseball a mile out the field. You sail toward a basketball goal like a winged angel. Did I say angel? But at night, in my kitchen, you swig down half a glass of milk, knock over the rest, and across the room, a whole quart of molasses swan dives to the floor. Mama warned me. She said, 'Christine, some days your children can strike a chord like B-flat gone sour.' I guess that day's here for me. I feel just like throwing in the towel."

And she did. Mom tossed the towel over her shoulder toward me. It landed *smack* into Amigo's face. Boy, did he ever suck on that milk and molasses. He pawed at his tasty toy, growled at it, flung it into the air. Hearing things, Mom began the task of pulling her curious self off the floor. That's when the wet towel landed at her feet. A sweet mess turned into a milk slide, and Mom slid. She landed toes up, her head slamming hard onto Grandma Edie's 1930's raised hearth.

Amigo ran to my mama's rescue. So did I. I begged, "Mom, wake up! Look at me! Please!"

In spite of the doggie's wet licks, Mom's eyelids failed to flicker. I called 911. The next number I dialed was Aunt Irene's. However, our neighbor, Mrs. White, raced over as soon as she saw the ambulance drive up. Amigo pressed in close to my legs.

Turns out, Mrs. White was a first-class neighbor. She said, "Danny, don't you worry about a thing. I'll take care of your house and your dog. What's his name?"

"Amigo," I told her.

I climbed into the ambulance's front passenger side and the driver started backing into the street. Mrs. White shouted, "See you at the hospital." Through that emergency vehicle's window my eyes followed Mrs. White.

She was herding Amigo through the doorway of her car garage. Gently, I noticed.

Next day when Aunt Irene arrived, Mom still lay unmoving in her ICU bed.

"I'm so glad you're here," I told my aunt.

I noticed her blue eyes looked a lot like Mom's, and dark circles beneath those eyes spoke of tiredness. Aunt Irene took my hand. She said, "Danny, where else would I be? You and Christine are my family!"

For days, Mom's *family* worried. In ICU, one minute Mom would wake up, I thought, as herself. The next, she'd turn senseless. Over and over she called for Daddy. One morning Mom looked at me and said, "Anson, bring me a beer."

A beer? Never in my life had I seen my mama drink beer!

Thankfully, two weeks later, Aunt Irene and I brought our patient home, and I was glad, for with no memory of that fateful morning, and her swelled up head still not quite shrunk to normal, I had feared the worst.

Throughout this ordeal, when verging on normal, Mom seemed to remember Dad, me, and Aunt Irene. One day Mom's gaze turned worried. She asked me, "Danny, does your Dad know about my accident?"

Aunt Irene answered the question. "I wrote him, Sis, but not until doctors told me they expected your complete recovery. Where he is, I didn't want him worrying."

The joyous day of Mom's homecoming, with Sister Irene to her left, and Danny Boy on her right, all three of us hospital depart-ers trudged up our front porch steps. I knocked on the door. I called, "Mrs. White! We're home!"

She must have been sweeping the floor or something. I feared Mom was tiring. I told her, "Mrs. White has been the best neighbor anyone could have asked for. She's been great help. "While you were in the hospital, most days she drove me to and from school. Oh, and you'll be glad to hear this. I passed my Shakespeare exam. I'm still on the basketball team."

Mom looked at me like, *What are you talking about?*

I know I told her about Coach Hamilton's Shakespeare conversation with Zack and me.

Guess that revelation leaked out of her memory bank.

Mrs. White opened the door. "Christine! Welcome home! We're glad you're better."

All the way home I'd worried. *How would Mom react, seeing Amigo.* Most nights when Grandma Edie tucked me in, she sat with me until I said my prayers. Riding in our car's back seat behind Aunt Irene and Mama I *became* a prayer. "Please, God, please, God, please, God," over and over and over. Waiting at our door, I thought, "Lord, it's now or never!"

Mrs. White stepped back, allowing my doggy friend fuller access to Mom. Amigo rushed to her side.

Mom's hands flew to her cheeks. My pre-accident mama shrieked "Son, we have a *dog*?"

Oh, oh! I helped Mom to her hearth chair. I held her hand. "You don't remember Amigo? That's sad. We love him a lot."

Mom stirred around in her chair, seeking comfort. Slightly dazed, she patted the doggie's head. "Cute little doggie, aren't you?" She turned to me. "Dan, Amigo looks hungry. What does he eat?"

I said, "Amigo's just crazy for milk and molasses, all mixed together."

Mom lifted her chin. She gestured to me. "Then bring him some." She bent as low as she could from her pillow-backed chair. She almost managed to rest her cheek against my friend's furry head. "I'm sorry I can't remember you, my doggie."

Her eyes darted toward me. "My dog? Amigo's *my* doggie?"

"Ours. Amigo's our dog," I told her.

Mom's face turned serious. "Danny, you and me, we need to start walking. Amigo would love that. Every day after school, until I find me a new job, let's -- you, me, and our doggie -- stretch our legs. It's not that far to the park. We can walk there, and back. My legs do need strengthening."

I hugged Mom. "Sounds great to me." *Thank you Lord!*

After Mrs. White went home and Aunt Irene helped Mom to bed, I took the leash I'd bought Amigo and fastened it to his new collar. Walking my and Mom's doggie up the sidewalk, I re-thought my view of Shakespeare. That English fellow had to have been one smart dude. Over three centuries ago he wrote a preview of what happened just today. He declared, "All's Well That Ends Well." And while neither Mom's, mine, nor Amigo's stories are anywhere close to ending, we're headed in the right direction, especially now that mean old Hitler's out of business. Last night, listening to Gabriel Heatter on the hospital radio, Aunt Irene and I let out a cheer. The newscaster said our soldiers should be coming home in nothing flat. I told my aunt, "Grandma Edie would have said they'd be home 'In a whip-stitch.'"

I say this: when the war ends, when Mom finds a job she likes, when Dad comes home with or without a job, when the four of us, Mom and Dad, Amigo and I, walk together to the park, my heart will sing, "All's Well That Ends Well!"

The Courtship of Maybelle
by Bert O. Richmond

Pretty Maybelle dwelled on a mountain high
Long flaxen hair and smooth, fair skin
Her eyes as blue
As the mountain sky
On a cloudless day.

She ran to her Pa one day
Face aglow like the morning sun
A smile as wide as the rest of her life
Bubbling, hurriedly told her Pa
I'm gettin' married to Jim-boy
Who lives on the creek down below.

Pa furrowed his brow
The love for his Maybelle
Shone fresh on his face
With eyes downcast, hesitatingly rebuked
You jest can't marry Jim-boy
My sweet only daughter
But never worry your pretty little head
'cause lots of young men
Will come asking for you.

Maybelle's face quickly altered
from joy to pain
As quick as the sky
pours out summer rain
Her tears started flowing
But why, Pa, why can't I marry Jim-boy?
I'm already seventeen
My girl-friends are married
Jim-boy is nineteen with a full-time job
No one our true love can rob.

Pa stammered, red-faced, spoke painfully slow
I was not always the man I am now
He hoped Maybelle would understand.
Jim-boy's momma and me
About 20 years ago
Took a shine to each other you see
Honey, Jim-boy is my son.

Sweet Maybelle ran from the room
That day
With hate for her Pa
Heart breaking from pain
Tears clouding the eyes of sky-blue
Her joy had turned to despair

Crying in pain
Consumed with shame

Tightly to her Ma she clung
The newly learned story on her tongue
Sobbed out her love for Jim-boy
A love she could now not fulfill.

Ma stroked her golden curls
Gazed into her azure eyes
Wiped away her flooding tears
I shoulda told you sooner
Since I'm your loving Ma
Don't worry, just marry your Jim-boy
'Cause you ain't no kin to Pa.

The Right Thing
by Elsa Russo

It was ten in the evening when the sounds of the small town had finally settled. The air was thick with humidity. A single car was slowly making its way down the street. It was the kind of car that people glance at, and then forget. That was part of the attraction to the person who was driving it. She had her dark hair tied in a tight bun on the back of her head. She leaned forward over the steering wheel and squinted through her wire-rimmed glasses at the road sign.

"I really need to get new glasses," she muttered.

"You've been saying that for three months now," said her companion in the passenger seat.

She was not a very small person, but she was small. She was even smaller in comparison to her companion. He was tall, muscular, and always ready for things to go wrong. He was loading a 9mm as they continued down the road.

"Remind me to make an appointment tomorrow," she said, squinting at the next road sign and making the turn.

"If we are still alive tomorrow," he said with a nod.

She rolled her eyes at him. "Could you be a little hopeful? Not so fatalistic? I do intend on both of us being alive tomorrow."

"You always intend on both of us being alive tomorrow."

"And have I been wrong yet?"

Her companion thought for a moment. Then he opened his coat and stuffed his gun into the holster. "Considering we are currently alive, no, you have not been wrong yet. But there's a first time for everything."

She let out an exasperated sigh and shook her head. "Why do I keep you around again?"

"I'm handsome."

"Just barely."

"I'm smart."

"You're dumb as a rock!"

"I'm dangerous."

"That I can attest to."

"And I am the best shot you have ever met."

She took in a breath and let out another deep sigh. "This is true."

A mischievous grin slowly widened on his face. "And I'm the best lay you've ever had."

She rolled her eyes. "Now you're just being an asshole."

He put his hand to his chest in mock shock. "What? I'm not?"

"We've never even slept together you mook!"

"Doesn't mean I'm not."

She rolled her eyes and put down her foot on the brake. "Here we go."

She put the car in park and turned off the ignition. Her companion looked out the window at the flower shop. "EVERYTHING MUST GO" read a sign across the door.

"He's going to be in the greenhouse in the back. I don't expect there to be any trouble," she said, as she turned off the car.

"You never expect trouble, but on this subject you're always wrong. There always is trouble."

"Not always."

He gave her a sidelong glance.

"Okay, vast majority of the time there is trouble. But at this stop I don't expect any." They both got out of the car. The girl went to the back of the car and unlocked the trunk. As it swung up, she glanced over the bags they had placed in the trunk three hours ago. She picked up the first one and shut the trunk with a quiet "click." Her companion had been standing on the sidewalk, staring at the door. She walked over and stood next to him.

"We're doing the right thing," she said quietly. "Just remember that."

"Are we?" he said, looking at her.

"Yes," she replied, staring straight back at him. "We are." She handed him the duffle bag. Then she took out her lock picks from her pocket. She crouched in front of the door and went to work. Her companion kept a lookout. She had only been working at it for ten seconds when the door flew open.

"What are you doing there?!" shouted an old man.

"Mr. Wallace," said the girl straightening up. "I'm sorry, I thought you were going to be out in your greenhouse."

"I was in my greenhouse!" His frizzy hair was illuminated by the lights of the store behind him and his thick glasses made his eyes look like a lizard's. Because he was so startled, his eyes looked even bigger and his cheeks were bright red as he shouted. "I was taking care of my orchids when my security camera showed me someone trying to break into my store at a particularly ungodly hour of the night! What are you doing here?!"

"We're bringing you this," said her companion, walking forward with the duffle bag in his hand.

"What's this?" Mr. Wallace unzipped the bag and stared dumbfounded at the stacks of cash in the bag. "What the hell is this?"

"You and several others in the community were scammed," said the girl.

He huffed. "What do you mean scammed?"

"A man going by the name of Greg Barnum came and offered you extra insurance that was specifically for florists and farmers. Once he had your bank account information, he took away your life savings. As a result, you couldn't pay your debts and you declared bankruptcy. Which I'm assuming is why you are also going out of business."

"Why I'm going out of business is none of your business!"

"Nevertheless. This is all the money that the man took from you."

Mr. Wallace looked at the bag, and then back at the two figures in front of him. "Is this a joke?"

The girl blinked. "No, this is…"

"What do you take me for – an idiot?! One man manages to swindle me so now everyone is out to get me?!"

"No, I just…"

"For all I know you were working with that man!"

The girl was starting to lose her temper now. "I wouldn't work for that cretin if it meant I would never go hungry again. Now please…"

"NO! Please, leave me alone!" He shoved the bag back at her companion and the door slammed back in their faces. The sound of the lock sliding into place was deafening on the quiet street.

The girl and her companion looked at each other. The man had one of his infuriating "told you so" looks on his face. The girl set her jaw and stared back.

"Well, surely the next one will actually believe us," she insisted.

"Sure, if that happens, I'll buy you a drink."

"And if it doesn't?"

"You buy me a drink. Lots of drinks."

After three more slammed doors, two threats of calling the police, and one very confused man, who thought they had been sent by a call girl agency he was waiting on, they were sitting on a curb next to the car. She was resting her chin in her hands and her partner was on his third beer of the six pack she had bought him on the way there.

"Don't look too sad, chérie," he said with a nudge. "You did try."

"I find out that Greg freaking Toombs, the worst scam artist I've ever met in my life, has bankrupted four gardeners and two farmers in this tiny town of ours. I use my knowledge gained from a sinful and wasted five years of my life spent with you…"

"Hey!"

"No offense."

"Mmm." He took a sip from his beer, still eyeing her suspiciously.

"I risk life, limb, reputation, credit rating, and my own computer equipment in order to get all the money back from that cheap, second-rate, insurance scam hacker, and now none of the people who were stolen from will take their money back. It's… ridiculous! It's insane!"

"It's the way people are."

She dropped her face into her hands with a heavy sigh.

"They've already been burned by one man with a plan that was too good to be true. Can you really blame them for not believing in yet another person who walks up to their doors with another plan that's too good to be true?"

She pushed her hair back from her face and pushed her glasses up her nose. "The reasonable part of my brain agrees with you. The part of my brain that wanted to actually do a good thing with all the dirty knowledge I've gained just wants to kick and scream until people realize that I'm actually trying to do something right."

"Keep trying to listen to the reasonable part of your brain there. That's the part that's going to get us out of this." Her companion gulped down what was left of his first beer and opened the second one.

"You're lucky it's so late," she sighed. "Otherwise the cops would be all over us for drinking in public. And then how in the world are we going to explain all those bags of money in the trunk?"

"We're Santa's elves?"

She smirked. Then she straightened up. By the look in her eyes he knew she had an idea. "What was the name of that detective who came snooping around last week?"

"Uh, hang on." Her companion began digging through his pockets. His fingers closed around a small card at the bottom of his suit coat pocket. He pulled it out and gave it out to her.

"Detective David Jackson," she said, reading it out loud.

"What exactly are you thinking?"

"Well, we can't keep the money. It doesn't belong to us. The longer we stay in this city, the more danger we are going to be in because by 8 am, Toombs is going to figure out that we're behind this."

"No, that *you're* behind this."

She looked at him with a bashful smile.

"Oh no, don't tell me you pulled me into this!"

"I couldn't do that many transactions under one of my pseudonyms. One of them had to be yours. Now, by 8 am, Toombs is going to be checking that account and he's going to discover that all the money he so carefully swindled is going to be gone. And he's probably going to recognize at least one of my pseudonyms."

"Which of my pseudonyms did you use?"

"Edmund Dantes."

Her companion looked a little more relieved now. "Oh, I barely use that one."

"Exactly. I doubt he'll trace that one. But he will probably trace Annie Oakley. He's seen that one I used at least once before."

"So, what is your plan?"

"I say, we give Detective Jackson a little Christmas present."

"How do you propose to do that?"

"Do you still have all that information we have on Toomb's accounts and how he used those to swindle the money out of people's accounts?"

"Yeah?"

"Let's get the money out of the trunk. I have a plan."

The next morning, Detective Jackson walked into his office to find a note sitting on his desk. He opened the note and read the following:

Detective Jackson,

Hello from your resident hackers, who are no longer your residents. Sorry to leave so abruptly, but once you see our office we're sure you'll understand. There are many things that we are comfortable doing. But we find the swindling and stealing of funds from people who have worked their whole lives at honest jobs to be unseemly. Because of that, we have left you a late Christmas present at our offices. Please make sure the money gets back to the people who deserve it. And please let them know that last night we were trying to do the right thing. Good luck! And we hope we never have to cross paths again.

Sincerely,

Bonnie and Clyde

At the bottom of the note was the address of the office they had been working in, along with a key that had been taped to the note. The detective was curious. So he went over to the address on the note with the key. He wasn't sure what he would find so he brought along his partner, Burns. They walked into the office and found six duffle bags sitting on an empty desk with a box on top. On the box was a note that said:

MERRY CHRISTMAS!

Jackson opened the box while Burns opened one of the duffle bags.

"Whoa..." said Burns, taking out two stacks of money. "If all of these have money in them... there has to be around..."

"$2,477,345, all told," said Jackson, staring at the figures sitting in front of him.

Burns' jaw dropped. "How did you..."

"They added it up for us."

"Bonnie and Clyde?"

"That's not the names I knew them by. But then they use pseudonyms so often I'm not sure if they ever use their real names. Even with each other."

Burns stared at the bags. "They stole all of this, didn't they?"

"Yep. And it was originally stolen from six hard-working individuals in town."

They stared at the bags and then at each other.

"Technically, we should arrest them," said Burns.

"Technically... I don't think we're ever going to find them." Burns nodded.

A few thousand miles away, the girl and her companion were sitting on a beach and staring up at the sun through dark sunglasses.

"Next time I say something like we should do the right thing, stop me," said the girl.

"Sure," he replied.

"You're not going to stop me, are you?"

"Have I ever been able to stop you from doing anything?"

She sighed and lay back on the sand. "Nope."

Tipsy Catastrophe Called Reuben
By Hannah King Thomas

It was a tipsy catastrophe called Reuben who knew how to look a lady in the eyes. Reuben, who had lines of soggy albums laid at your eyes like tile and Reuben, who asked you to pick one—you know, Reuben. Reuben, who had your universe hanging on your arm, after he'd placed it there, and Reuben, who didn't need a tin cup or an old can to catch that you didn't think he did anything to deserve your money. Reuben, he'd look to you and to the continual others to pass him and have every distrustful appendage you had on your handbag, and to pretend that you already had too many soggy albums to add another—you, you didn't have a single soggy album, did you—but Reuben, it didn't bother him to bow anyhow and make his way of life into an existential industry that skimmed people's insides for just under ten minutes and then sent them off to make literature of him, Reuben.

Reuben, you did right! Reuben, you put the universe on my right arm (that isn't right, it was my left). You put my universe where it mattered most. My universe stumbled on his chuckles with blushes but watched our fall unfold all the same, and my universe watched you, Reuben, and you watched two people who will infinitely be blissfully in love by your memory, Reuben. Reuben, who's told you you did right before?

Reuben, you did right.

And sober people are a sordid sort and an old attraction. They have no candor! They're hand-me-down happy; who among them has honestly given a long thought to not wasting away in the wanton way they make on? They may have filed unthinkingly into sobriety and they may have never manhandled well-heckled handouts, but they didn't think to drape my universe long on my left side—they didn't think to say any impatient baits to make me take a soggy album, they didn't think to blink the unfamiliarity of me or the others of the street away, they didn't think to make a friend or a mark alike! But my—Reuben, you did, and Reuben, you did right.

Reuben, I couldn't quit you if I wanted to, Reuben. I'll keep with the going and write a whole saga with you, for you saw what few did, you did, and you were the witness that the sixth of November needed, and I'll believe in you like I believe in being brokenhearted henceforth, and hosting the imposition of happiness only when it visits me.

He was all of ten minutes of a man. Reuben was made with merely ten minutes on the mind, that's all the divine had designed his capacity to withstand. He lived increments of repetition with little depth and little width, with little interactions that set his sea level just to the tip of his brim, and then doused out the tidal canister in his head with drainage. He wore filth like a primary color. He lived with his back to a wall, watching. His teeth didn't deign to listen to you, or turn to you when they or you talked; they faced each other or they didn't come to your call at all, inapparitions that had better places to be than gums kissed with gristle. He drank frantically for someone or one of their things to extend the slim ten minutes of time he'd been given to live, and when he saddled up next to your or my side, when he flogged tirelessly the sales pitch for the sake of soggy albums, it was really for what he was imploring, some extension or some end of the endless meaninglessness. He meant what he said, and to his eyes that made twins of his vision, you really were the most beautiful girl in the world, and he wanted your universe to know it. Reuben.

Left Hand
by Alan Curtis

The shy brother who never shakes
At parties. Sometimes hides behind a back,
Or wrapped around a balcony rail,
Supports a leaning body,
While the other raises a glass.

It patiently holds the plate,
But never grasps the knife.
It clears a space at the table,
For the other to rest its load.
Touches the cheek chastely,
While the other delves among warm curves.
Holds still the patient,
Whiles the other wields the blade.
Thoughtfully strokes a beard,
While the other moves the pen.

But when the guitar is uncased,
The left leaps forth,
Fingers tapping down the frets,
Fluid as Astaire down a staircase.
Rapid notes sparking into melodies,

While the other plucks and strums,
Mutely following the dancing left.

But come the applause,
The right hand waves,
Accepting the plaudits,
And stealing the bow,
While the left grips the instrument
Tightly by the neck.

The New Math at the New School
by DJ Thomason

TEACHER: Welcome to class this morning. I hope you had a great weekend. And since this is Monday, we will say the pledge of allegiance. Everyone stand who wishes to stand.

[Edgar stands]

TEACHER: Thank you, Edgar. The rest of you may remain sitting, but please imagine that you're standing in your minds. Now repeat after me. "I pledge allegiance to my happiness. I am me. I am good." Great. Everyone can sit back down.

[Edgar sits.]

TEACHER: Today we will continue our math and grammar class, which, as you know, has been combined in the new curriculum because of obvious similarities in structure. I will write on the chalkboard, and that information will be sent to your iPads, which, thanks to the new Cerebella Sync Adapters, will be beamed into your brains, allowing you to continue staring into the distance and daydreaming.

[On the board, she writes:]

Use the following base components to calculate:

16 x 16 = what?

Base components:
To and too equals for
For and fore equals ate
Ate and too equals tin

Answer:
16 equals too times ate, which is too less than tin, so take too tins, take away won fore. Do that twinny times, take away fore times and you get 182.

EDGAR: I just punched it into my calculator and it came out to be 256.

TEACHER: It doesn't have to be exact, Edgar. The numbers we get in our computations do not have to match what you get with a calculator.

VOICE FROM THE BACK: I got 256, too, using straight multiplication.

TEACHER: Principal Perkins, please refrain from hiding in the back of the room and causing trouble. Please leave. Thank you.

EDGAR: May I go to the bathroom?

TEACHER: Edgar, there is a proper way and an improper way to ask questions. Yours was the archaic and improper way. You should say, CAN I go to the bathroom? MAY implies that you're asking my permission, which would give me authority over you, which is wrong in human society. Who taught you to say it that way?

EDGAR: My grandfather.

TEACHER: Please refrain from listening to your grandfather. Apparently, he is too old to understand modern societal values.

EDGAR: CAN I go to the bathroom?

TEACHER: Of course. Anyone else need to go to the bathroom? A female, preferably, since we don't want anyone to infer that we're unfairly allowing one gender to go over another. Sabrina? Brittany?

[Ellie raises her hand]

TEACHER: Thank you, Ellie.

[Teacher picks up small device from desk}

TEACHER: Now I'm going to activate the Cerebella Sync.

[Presses button on small device]

TEACHER: Okay. Did everyone receive that? Did anyone NOT

receive the lesson? Okay, good. Next on the agenda……does anyone want to take a selfie with the chalkboard which is showing today's lesson? No? Okay, does anyone want to take a selfie with me? That's great. Please form a line. Sabrina, please pull your shirt back down. We're in school, not Victoria's Secret. Anybody got any lipstick I can borrow? Duck lips look better with lipstick. Thank you, Robert.

An Ode to a Tissue
by Seth Monyette

Achoo!

~ Why, bless you ~

~ Why, thank you ~

Have you the flu?

No, I don't believe I do!

A tissue?

No thank you.

I promise it is brand new.

No thank y-

But your face, it's covered in goo!

I'm fine... jeez, leave me be will you?

...

...

...

I've not known someone to refuse a tissue after a sneeze before...

Whatever is the god-damned matter with you?

You sniveling, sniffling fool.

I hate you. I hate you I do.

You belong in a zoo, you're a goddamned animal.

Damn you.

Damn you to hell.

No respect...absolutely none...I can't believe that... it isn't believable, really...

...

...

...

Alright, I got that loser to leave now let rehearsals continue.

Has everyone brought their kazoo?

DOO DOOO DOOOO!!!!!!

Indeed, the kazoos, you have them, you do.

"What Is... Alex Trebek?"
by Seth Monyette

It was a beautiful evening. My lovely wife and I had just reached the peak of laughter for the entire night. Tears were streaming down each of our faces, like a waterfall flows with its salty salt water. The golden sun beat down on our faces like a pounding, pounding drum. Except it was pleasant, so maybe, actually, it was more like a gentle tapping of a drum. The golden sand shone brightly, reflecting the sun's glare into my partner's sunglasses, wherein I could see the most handsome man in the world – MYSELF. I stole a quick sip from my pina colada, a sexy gesture at that, I was sure.

Hannah, my significant other, gazed at me with her alluring glare. She said, "What a beautiful evening. I particularly enjoyed the way we shared that moment in which we guffawed so loudly and for so long, that even the waves themselves rumbled with their own laughter in response."

"Haha!" I replied. I didn't really hear what she said so I took the liberty of assuming that it was a joke.

A deep rumble shook the Earth. My colada flew from my hands into mid-air... and there... it floated. Whatever appears to be happening here? Are coconuts not subject to the law known as gravity? Not quite a law anymore I suppose. I quickly snap my attention to my wife. A new reflection appears in her sunglasses. What could she be gazing at? I squinted harder – it was unmistakable. Those brilliant and gleaming spectacles snoozing upon his nose, that unforgettable bright white light emanating from his mane, the rippling, meaty muscles – veiny as can be. Yes, it was definitely Alex Trebek. One three-quarter turn to my right later, I was face to face with the man. Intimidation overcame me.

"Contestant, what is your name?" His voice was like a lion's roar atop of a mountain, echoing on and on into infinity.

"Contestant. What is your name?" he repeated, even more majestic than before.

I froze. What to reply with?!

"Contestant, what is your name?? Con…"

I jolted awake from my deep slumber.

"Carl, wake up for work! Carl, wake up for work!"

"I'm up! I'm up!" I replied, while hopping out of bed and wiping the sleep from my eyes.

"What kinda dream were you havin' huh? Kickin' an moanin' all over the bed," Hannah asked.

I sighed deeply. "I saw him again."

"Oh no."

"He's in my dreams now, too?! When does it end?! Where does it end, Hannah?" In a fit of rage, I clenched my hands into balls of fist and flung my arms violently outwards. My bedside lamp in turn suffered a blow and fell to the floor with a crash.

"Look… sweetie… it'll be okay…" She had no idea where to even begin consoling me. We both knew, and so we embraced.

***

Fully dressed head to toe, I was looking good and feeling better. I had on my finest slacks, a baby blue long sleeve shirt that reminded me of home, my finest blazer and the crown jewel – my great grand papa's very special tie. It was an old tie, and it smelled like old things do. You know, just generally not good. Antique? No, it was not antique. It was bad. It smelled bad. Even still, I looked great – a boost of confidence that I truly needed if I were to make it through the day without losing my sanity.

HONK! A horn honked at me. I didn't like that.

"C'mon!" I yelled.

This accomplished nothing of course, and so I continued on with my way to work. Times Square was absolutely bustling, as busy as always. Above me and straightforward, *he* spoke.

"Choose the right brand. Use your head, America."

A chorus of hushed, yet clearly audible, whispers followed. "New Nike AirGlydes – from Alex Trebek."

"Yes. It *is* the finest product yet. Yes. Don't hesitate. *Yes*."

In extreme close-up, I could see the single drop of sweat resting on his handsome brow. "Nike AirGlydes. Why wait to have them later when you could own them now?"

To my immediate left, three separate ads rolled: McDonalds, Cover Girl and The New York Times. He chomped into a triple-decker cheeseburger and spoke only after he had eloquently patted his mouth with his napkin, and then returned it safely back to his lap. "This is Alex Trebek introducing the McBek Burger, the tastiest burger in America. Critics are raving." Reviews with 10/10 stars flew all about the screen, too fast to even read.

He strutted down a fashion runway, deserted, and blindingly white, nearly rendering his hair invisible. Addressing the camera directly as he walked, he spoke. "If you're not using Cover Girl, then you're just not covering... girl. Introducing Trebëch perfume, featuring hints of rosë, lemon, and notes of Alex Trebek's own, personal musk."

He was seated in his study reading a newspaper, completely engaged. The story must have been gripping. He pressed his spectacles further up his nose ever so carefully, what was *this*, three-quarters to his right? Oh, a camera! He smiles right at me, and I feel something inside me melt like butter in a microwave. The New York Times? *That's* what Trebek reads? Oh well. I should grab a cop - No! No, no, no! I can't let him control me this way!

I whipped around and there I was face-to-face with a three-story-high screen. "BROADWAY THEATRE PRESENTS: SEXIEST MAN OF THE YEAR WINNER - ALEX TREBEK." What the hell would his performance even be anyways? He can't entertain that many people on his own for very long! Oh, who was I kidding? I would love to see such a tremendous event. It would be talked about for generations and I could say, "Hey! I was there! I saw Trebek on Broadway!" No! I must try my best to avoid Trebek. I tucked my head down. *I will not look upwards*, I told myself, and continued to walk. Not five-and-a-half steps in and below me, I spotted: "PLAYGIRL Model of the Year – Alex Trebek. What is… the sexiest man alive?" GODDAMMIT! I quickened my pace. Over the span of fifteen seconds of speed walking, I see Trebek's face at least six more times. Had I actually seen this many pictures of Alex lying on the ground? Or was he just in my head? Was I seeing him when I closed my eyes, too? Can I escape?!

TREBEK TREBEK TREBEK TREBEK TREBEK TREEBECK TREEBARK. GET. OUT. OF MY HEAD!!!!!!!!

I lifted my gaze from the ground, and the realization hit me that I just walked as quickly as possible through Times Square without looking where I was going. Have you ever been struck by a car?

A daze. My vision – blurred. Hazy. Foggy. Boggy. Sloggy. Goggy. Soggy Doggy. Where was I? And that voice? It's so far away…but so familiar.

"is…-rrect…!"

"Wh-… cheese…six-hun-…"

DING!!!

My vision focuses. A screen hangs from the ceiling above. Mostly a dark hue of blue within, but various shapes as well. Person-type shape... oh, they're people. Right. It was utter beauty. There is no better way to awaken; I don't care who you are, or what you believe in. But on this we can agree, it is undeniably the best way to be greeted back into the world. Also, my arm was broken. Hurt like shit. Oh, and my wife was standing next to me. Wife? Is that right? Is this my wife? Hilton? What's her name? Is it me she is talking to? Forget it, not important. Trebek is on the screen, speaking to me. I make out small bits of what my wife, Harby, says, but man oh man, was she boring.

"...can't afford to... sorry...just tha-...want this?... John?...if you don't answer then..."

Who cares, Hillary? Quit whining and leave me alone to my sweet, sweet Trebek.

"Fine, then... I'm sorry... I know you would do the same... Doctor." She nods.

I raised my head, and the realization hit me that I just ignored the words someone was speaking to me when I probably should have listened.

Have you ever died before?

Believe you, me, when they say "pull the plug," this doesn't refer to the television, not at all. No. I wouldn't have been okay with either one being pulled in my hospital room, but this particular plug... this might be worse than the television plug. Oh well, deal with the hand you're given. That is my motto after all, and so I approached the luminous golden gates, figuring hey, why not?

The receptionist at the gate was a witch. I supposed it was probably just the look she gave me, specifically those glasses. No, it was just those damned glasses. I figured it mostly had to do with the sharp points on either side's outer rim. Two painstaking hours later (outrageous that there was no available Wi-Fi I mean really...), it was my turn. My moment of glory. I strode some fifty yards towards the gates and there, St. Peter stood patiently. I shed a single tear.

"Are you cool?" he questioned me.

I was flustered, "Uh... yeah... I guess...I...yeah ...dude... I'm cool."

"Very well," he said as the gates flung open backward.

There before me stood the one true King of Kings. The one to rule them all. The head honcho. The boss. The big man himself. The white light was blinding. Tears streamed endlessly down my face, my emotions beyond my control. Beauty, in its rawest, purest of forms, is not often seen by man. So, when a man truly sees it, he will know. He will know. And so I knew... that this was beauty. True beauty.

"Alex. I can't believe it's really you..." I managed to speak, as I crumbled in his glory. Alex Trebek ... was God all along.

The E-Mail Caper
by Donna McGinty

"What is it?" Alice Flynn cast a sidelong look at the object her son had deposited on her kitchen counter next to a Mr Coffee drip machine.

Jeff smiled and placed the palm of his hand on the object's smooth gray surface. "It's a gift, Mom…a laptop computer."

He'd arrived before she'd finished her first cup of coffee and the crossword puzzle, an interruption that most often sharpened her tongue. But he was beaming, and she decided to let him down gently. She backed up a step and tightened the belt of her bathrobe.

"Well, thank you son, but why do I need a…a computer? You should give it to Madison."

Jeff's smile faded. "Madison's computer is top-of-the-line. It could run her college or, damn near, run the Pentagon."

"Don't swear, son. And watch those clichés."

"I'm sure the army of English majors you sent into the world have never sullied their speech or writing with a cliché."

Alice smiled. "Do I detect some peeve and sarcasm?"

He sighed and counted to ten. "Okay. Let's start over. I'm running behind. Flying to Dallas after lunch and won't get back until Friday late. So come sit with me a minute and finish your coffee. I'll explain."

He led her by the elbow to the cherry table and pulled out a chair. He sat across the table and waited until she'd sipped cold coffee and set down the mug.

"Mom, you have to help Jenna and me with our time crunch. If you'd learn e-mail…well, our communications would go smoother and faster. You understand? You do know how e-mail works, don't you?"

She studied him with pale blue eyes magnified by soda-bottle lenses acquired decades ago after cataract surgery. "What," she said carefully, "does this e-mail have that U.S. mail lacks?"

"Speed. If you need me, I'll know instantly."

"Then I'll just call you. Last time I checked, the telephone is instant communication."

"Not if I'm on a conference call or in a dragged out staff meeting. Besides, you can't copy Jenna on the telephone like with e-mail."

"Son, you know how I feel about all this newfangled technology. Should be enough I let you talk me into an answering machine and this…this quite unnecessary panic-button." She touched the white object hanging from her neck. "But, Jeff—"

"Mother, stop! No buts, please." He pulled on the knot in his tie. The house was too warm, battling with the crisp October air outside. "I'm begging you to learn e-mail and use it. It won't be difficult. You still have all your…your faculties."

Alice clapped her hands and laughed, head thrown back. "You almost said *marbles*, didn't you?"

His look of confusion gave way to a headshake. "Don't avoid the issue. You write lovely letters but that's no way—"

"Hush! Just hush, son. Your father and I wrote long letters to each other until the day he died. Solved many an argument that way. Never went to bed angry."

"I know, Mom, but times have changed. You need to help me. Please. I can only handle so much."

"Oh, I know, and I'm sorry. If only I could still drive, I could help more."

"But you can't drive. What you *can* do is quit being stubborn and learn e-mail."

Her cheeks flushed, and she studied the tabletop. After a few moments, she looked up with magnified eyes and blinked. "Very well. I can't stand to disappoint you. Didn't like to disappoint your father either. Will you teach me?"

Jeff let out a held breath. He stood, leaned over, and kissed her forehead. "Thank you. But I don't have the time or patience. I've lined up one of my best employees—Sid—to spend the afternoon with you. He's a great instructor. By the time he leaves you'll be e-mail savvy."

She waved him off and picked up the crossword puzzle. "Tell Sid not to come a minute before one-thirty. I need my beauty rest after lunch."

***

On Friday, Jeff's flight home from Dallas arrived on time, twenty minutes before heavy rain and lightning left planes circling the Atlanta airport. He checked the time on his iPhone. If luck held, and traffic moved, he could make it to the office in time to consult Sid.

Forty minutes later he was safely parked under the building and climbing the stairs, two at a time, to the second floor. His secretary didn't see him until he stepped into the office. She hesitated in the middle of pulling on a jacket that matched the red of the Kate Spade purse propped on a desk chair. He stopped in front of her. She smiled and handed him a stack of pink slips—telephone calls.

"I hope," she said, "you don't mind if I leave fifteen minutes early. The rain—"

"No. No. But first, round up Sid, if he's still here."

He waited impatiently at his desk, sneaking peeks at the papers and file folders stacked high in the inbox. Five minutes later, a smiling Sid arrived, coat on, car keys hooked on a forefinger. Jeff was envious he couldn't summon the weekend energy infecting his staff. He sighed and looked at Sid.

"So how did it go with my mother?"

Sid gave a thumbs-up. "We had a bumpy start. Said she was still groggy from a nap. But, hey, I didn't get the boot. Stayed all afternoon. Even got treated to cookies."

"But, damn it, did she learn to use e-mail?"

"Yeah. That lady's got all her marbles." He laughed. "And I learned that I can't talk without using clichés."

"But do you know she can actually do it—send and receive messages? She hasn't e-mailed me."

"When I left, I asked her to practice on me. Waited hours. About to give up then—boom—there it was, an e-mail. Gotta admit the message cracked me up, and not a typo in sight." He grinned. "You'll never guess what she wrote, boss."

"Then, damn it, tell me so you can get your weekend underway."

"Hmm, okay. Real neat sentence it was. *The quick brown fox jumped over the lazy dog's back.* That was it. No hello. No goodbye."

Jeff shrugged. "Sounds like my mother's quirky sense of humor."

"Yeah, she's got that all right. Showed up in the e-mail address she came up with. You ready? *SonsIdea234@* gmail.com."

Jeff waved a hand. "Go on, get outta here, Sid. Have a good weekend."

***

When Jeff got home he found his wife, Jenna, asleep on the couch in the family room, the evening news playing softly on the wall-mounted

TV. When she didn't stir, he went to the master bedroom and dropped his carry-on on the king bed. With it unzipped, he carefully sorted items to be washed or dry-cleaned. Then he changed into sweats and walked quietly to the kitchen. He uncorked a bottle of Pinot Grigio and was pouring a glass when Jenna came in, rubbing her eyes.

"I'm glad you're home." She put her arms around his neck and they kissed lightly.

"Me too."

"Honey, let's enjoy the weekend." She stepped back and searched his face. "You seem down. Did Sid bomb with Alice?"

"No, but she hasn't e-mailed me yet. I'm the mouse and my mother's the cat."

"Or you could finally accept my scenario." She poured herself a glass of wine.

"I know, I know. She's just trying to assert herself, hang on to her independence. But I wish she wouldn't center her resistance in last century's modes of communication."

Jenna smiled, took Jeff's hand, and led them toward the family room. "You have to admit, she writes a good letter."

***

Saturday morning before breakfast, Jeff checked e-mail. Nothing from his mother. He clenched a fist on the keyboard. He'd be damned if he'd cave and e-mail first. After breakfast, he tamped his growing irritation by tackling Jenna's honey-do-list, while she put on the wash. For lunch, he suggested they go to the neighborhood bistro but she declined, so instead they ate delivered veggie pizza while sitting on stools at the bar just off the kitchen.

Mid-afternoon, Jeff swept two inches of red, yellow, and scarlet leaves off the back wrap-around deck and readied the grill for cooking salmon later. When he couldn't amuse himself with chores any longer, he sat at his computer and scanned the latest e-mails. There it was. The first modern communication from his mother.

He opened her e-mail and read the subject line: *Welcome home, son.* He felt a tingle of pride, as a blank subject line was a pet peeve. Sid's instruction had been thorough. For another few moments, he kept his gaze off the body of the message and savored sweet victory. When curiosity took over, he focused on the one-line message, and his face quickly reddened.

She'd written: *Jeff, please check your mailbox for a letter. Love, Mom*

Hives
by Charles Beacham

(Note to readers: Some sections of this story contain graphic material)

 I feel it coming. The warmth grows inside my belly like a small fire ignited by a tribe of sand gnats camping in my intestines. I've felt it before—three times to be exact—but figured it wouldn't visit tonight. I try to ignore it, deny the rising—check email, smoke a cigarette, pet the dog for the fifth time in two minutes—but I can't sit still. A two-headed snake emerges from my intestines and slithers toward my crotch. One head lifts and rises toward my belly and chest and brain, the other descends to my legs and feet.

 Dana hollers from the kitchen, "Can I get anything for you?"

 I say, "No, I'm okay." But really, I'm panicked over the speed and volume at which blood is racing through my veins. The tribe has morphed into an army and advances.

 Keenly am I aware of every inch of my body. Each heartbeat pulses my skin. Every nerve ending ignites. In unison, they flash like a universe of small-town traffic lights at four in the morning. I wish I hadn't thrown away my television because it was a distraction, because at the moment, distraction is exactly what I need. I think about ESPN and Comedy Central and all those commercials I'm missing.

 I don't want to believe it and flip through excuses in my head. *Hemorrhoids?* No, can't be. Herbal ointment took care of those. *Ah, what's the use pretending?* I can't deny it any longer. I shouldn't have eaten the lamb tonight, which sucks, because I really enjoy The Mirage, the only Middle Eastern restaurant in town.

The skin below my butt crack is on fire, the part between my dumper and family jewels. I must scratch—it's the only way to soothe the burn. But I know from experience that one scratch will cascade into others, and the fire will spread, an army of ants ravaging my flesh, erecting mounds between my bones and skin. I scratch, long witch-nails scraping frosted glass. The assault could last for hours, unless I do something now.

"It's happening again, honey," I say to Dana. "I didn't want to think it was happening, but it is."

She peers around the corner from the kitchen with a mixture of smirk and concern on her face. "What's happening?"

"The skin tucked under the jewels is itching, Honey, burning."

And that's the first sign. Well, the first sign is heat in the belly, but that's more a precursor.

Dana's dealt with this before. The first time was just after we landed in Lima. I blamed cleaning chemicals because the first thing I did after clearing customs was take a big dump in a freshly sanitized bathroom.

Damned chemicals.

We walked around Miraflores for two hours searching for a pharmacy. It didn't matter when we found one because neither of us could read over-the-counter bottles in Spanish.

Damn Americans.

Finally, we found a twenty-four hour grocery store, which would surely have oatmeal, at least. While she deciphered labels, I writhed in the middle of the aisle, recoiling from the heat pulsing my brain, convinced I would pass out right there on the floor.

But I didn't. We made it back to the hostel and I sat in a cold bath of oatmeal for as long as I could stand it. Afterward, I lay in bed shivering in a daze, hypnotized by fake blondes with canyon cleavage on Peruvian TV, even though I didn't understand what the hell they were talking about. The burning was gone when I woke the next morning. *Thank you, Jesus.* I felt bloated, but we were on vacation, and I didn't want to ponder it again.

"Guess you shouldn't have eaten the lamb," Dana says, her neck tilted to the side, brown locks cascading over a shoulder. A smile perched on her face.

I lift one leg to the ceiling and launch a hand to my crotch. *Ah, feels so good to scratch.*

"We checked," I remind her. "Sulfites aren't used in lamb."

She agrees. "Add lamb to the list. Lamb, steak, honey-baked ham."

The night after Thanksgiving, I had woken engulfed, scratching my limbs and trunk in an unending procession of parts. The fire burned hotter, deeper than in Lima. The army had increased its ranks. I launched upright, but couldn't climb out of bed alone.

We were at Dana's parents' house and her dad wouldn't take kindly to me standing naked in the hallway moaning and excavating my crotch. He'd call her after we left and ask, "Why are you bringing this Neanderthal to my house for Thanksgiving?" Her dad's good at coming up with such descriptors.

I woke her, saying, "It's back," as if a little girl was standing before a fuzzy TV screen.

Dana didn't understand what I meant, but woke to help anyway. I appreciate her for doing it, and she knows I'd do the same for her. Luckily, we never spend the night at my parents' house.

She crept into the kitchen, not wanting to alert her parents to the human welt she'd brought home for Thanksgiving. She found a package of oatmeal and drew a bath while I flailed on the floor.

"Much better than Miraflores," I proclaimed. "Make the water as warm as possible." And I believed it, until she said, "Warm water only inflames the hives."

In the moment, it didn't matter to me. I didn't want to freeze my ass off, again.

"We should get some Benadryl," she said. "So if this happens again, we'll be ready."

I said, "Guess it wasn't the chemicals in Lima."

She said, "Nope."

Turns out, the chemicals didn't cause the hives in Lima after all. Instead, the culprit was the miniature beef patty I ate on the last leg from Panama City with a minuscule side of microwaved mashed potatoes.

Damned airplane food.

"This time, the ham sandwich you ate before bed caused it. You must be allergic to sulfites, or another preservative. We'll have to research it further."

She was right on two accounts. Each time it happens, new clues emerge.

"Damn honey-baked ham sandwich," I said. "We ate a delicious vegan Thanksgiving meal, and I topped it off with ham. No more ham for me."

"Or bacon," she added.

I huffed and puffed and sloshed around the tub. Bacon pulled me from vegetarianism a decade ago and reminds me of Nana's house. Now, I'd be leaving the salty, greasy goodness behind again. Only this time, not by choice.

Earlier in the evening, when we still believed common preservatives to be the culprits, Dana read that sulfites aren't used to preserve lamb. She checked specifically before we drove across town to The Mirage. Now, my mind wonders: *What else could it be?*

The fire line's ascending my torso now. It creeps through my sternum, but I know the army's also assaulting my sides and back. I attack my belly with furious fingernails, leaving trails of lava sizzling across my skin. For a second, I feel relief, but the fire rekindles. I dance with the flames: *scratch, relief, burn, scratch, relief, burn.* As the choreography unfolds, the fire spreads, so that more body parts are engulfed and demand scratching. Again and again, they'll fester, spread, and combine with each other until the inferno swallows me whole.

"Do we have any Benadryl?" I ask Dana. The possibility sparks a twinge of hope.

"I don't know," she says. "We should've checked before now." She laughs.

I join her. It's funny—sitting here helpless—morphing into red Goliath-sized welts.

"Check the medicine cabinet."

She hustles down the hallway to check.

If we have any, it probably expired in 1999, but that doesn't matter. I know expiration dates are a marketing ploy anyway. Plus, it's the only thing in the house that could offer relief. The inferno is aiming for my throat now, the army trying to sizzle my breath and steal my voice. She comes back wearing a sad face and shakes her sculpted jaw.

Thank God Dana's a nurse; she'll think of something. She's crafty. That's one thing I really like about her. She checks both bathrooms, rifles through the cabinets, but returns empty-handed. We sulk together—me in fiery agony, her in frustration at the inability to extinguish the blaze.

She asks, "Do you have a first aid kit in your hiking pack?"

I scratch my hips and chest before answering her question because it's a chore to think when my skin's blazing from head to toe. Though the embers are in the process of melting my sternum, I eek out a thought. Surprisingly, words follow.

"You're fucking brilliant!" I stagger to the hall closet and fling camping gear from the pack into the hallway until I spot the first aid kit.

I return excitedly, like a toddler who just completed his first unassisted poop. As she shuffles through the kit, I sit in the recliner with my legs pointed at the ceiling, grunting while the troops continue colonizing my body. She finds Benadryl in the kit, a packet containing two twenty-five milligram pills.

"Expired 2004," she reads.

"At least it's within a decade," I say, scratching my neck, and jaw, and hairline.

The invaders have planted their flags on every part of my body. The insides of my elbows pulse and flash, the lobes of my ears drip like liquid wax from a candle. I am the candle. I imagine my ears elongated like the Buddha's, except mine don't hang towards peace, but to escape the onslaught of histamine.

"Can I take both pills?" I ask, dreaming of an antihistamine daze.

"Let's see how you do with one," she says, tearing the package.

I snarl, but it only makes the corners of my mouth itch, so I get to scratching them.

"Open up," she says, and plops the twenty-five milligrams of paradise into my mouth.

As the rancid chemical dissolves, I pray it will extinguish the fire. She hands me a half-full glass of water and I slam it down. Steam rises from my throat as the water plummets into the seething cauldron of my belly.

"Let's get you into the bath," she says, and motions to the hallway.

From inside a burning bush, I peer at her, the way Jehovah did after presenting Moses with the first tablet of commandments. "I don't feel like taking a bath."

"You'll feel better, like in Lima or at Mom and Dad's. At least come back and relax on the bed."

I want to ask, "How in the hell am I supposed to relax when my fucking body's on fire?"

But I don't.

Instead, I wobble to my feet like the Kool-Aid man and swerve down the hallway toward the bedroom. I swear flames are trailing off my back, but when I turn around to look, they disappear. Flopping onto the California king, I try to relax, to meditate into calm.

But those pink mounds rising demand attention. They connect to each other like mountains did when they emerged and formed chains so long ago. The next thirty minutes morph into frenzy. Starting at my throat, my nails plow across my entire body. When every inch of skin has been raked, the procession begins again.

Finally, the Benadryl kicks in—the top layer of skin cools. My head floats up to the ceiling fan. The fire remains, but I'm just a little less compelled to scratch the itch. I settle onto a pile of pillows and scratch hot spots intermittently. The Benadryl worked, or maybe, I realize, I'm barely surviving in slow motion, still mining skin like a pot of gold is buried under there.

"The skin's the largest organ of the body," she says.

With rubbery lips, I mumble, "Don't remind me." I feel each little throbbing pore, every hair, every nerve and blood vessel, like one of those cartoons who stuck his finger in a light socket.

Dana's staring at her laptop screen now. "I think I found

something," she says.

Her voice reaches my ears, but the Benadryl is mesmerizing my brain, turning her words into some type of ancient code. The devil has reached my eyelids and they swell to half-shut. I don't even bother scratching anymore.

Her mouse scrolls, though I'm too busy imagining myself as a useless sack of inflamed skin on the bed. But then she says something that grabs my attention. What's left of my ears perk up.

"Listen to this! Here's a man who gets hives after eating red meat. For five years, he tried to figure out the cause. When his doctor ran allergy tests, he discovered a reaction to ticks. Seems the antibody created for lone star tick bites in some human bodies reacts to a carbohydrate in mammalian meat called galactose-alpha-1,3-galactose—Alpha-gal for short."

The genesis of a different bulge draws my attention. "You know it turns me on, honey," I mumble through the haze, "when you use big scientific words."

She giggles and says, "When Alpha-gal enters this man's body, histamine is released to battle it like a tick bite."

I sense relief. Perhaps she discovered how to avoid spontaneous combustion in the future. I reach for her hand, craving the caress of her long fingers.

"No more red meat for you," she says.

I kiss her hand with my bulging rubber lips and cross the threshold to antihistamine dreams.

You Dirty Bird!
by Jim Murdock

Rube awoke early on his wedding day. Confusing thoughts had played in his mind throughout the night. He really loved Kristy and felt guilty that thoughts of Amy kept entering his mind. She had been his first love, but now those feelings had to be set aside. Most upsetting were his memories of Cousin Caresse. Was that love or another feeling just as powerful? No one must ever know about that.

Would the Blankenschipf curse be present at the wedding? He wondered.

His mother, Betty, and Aunt Lucille prepared a large breakfast of eggs, grits, gravy, biscuits, jelly, sorghum molasses, orange juice and coffee for the family.

When Rube arrived at the table, David asked, "Are you nervous, Rube?"

"Of course not. This is only the most important day of my life. Everything's under control," boasted Rube.

"Then why is your fly open?"

Rube corrected the problem. "Just a small glitch," he said.

Uncle Billy sat at one end of the table with a bit of shaving cream clinging to one ear. His wrist was a little sore. Ellie was fine. They talked of Rube's visit to Dallas and Mr. Bennett's visit.

Remembering the story Uncle Billy used to tell, Rube asked, "How's the fascist, Uncle Billy?"

"He's fine. Still acts up every now and then. Rattles his chain and makes noise." They all laughed as he continued, "Rube, I want you to know that the fascist's feelings were hurt that he didn't receive an invitation to the wedding."

"Oh, I'm sorry about that. I couldn't have him disrupt the wedding by dragging his chains down the aisle. Besides, who would want to sit next to him?"

"You have a point there, my boy. I'll give him your regrets when I get back to Dallas."

The young people winced as Calvin said, "Billy, would you please give our blessing?"

"Yes, but first we must hold hands." He proceeded to bless the family, naming each member: the President, the Vice President, the Congress, the Supreme Court, the State of Georgia, the Flag, American soldiers all over the world, the peacemakers of the world, Kristy's family, the church where they would be married, the preachers and everyone in the wedding party.

When he got through all the names, Ellie said, "Daddy! You forgot to bless the food!"

"Okay, bless the food. Amen."

David piped in with, "I hate to say it Daddy, but you also forgot the table cloth and silverware."

They laughed and began devouring the lukewarm food.

Cal Munson picked Rube up at 12:30 p.m. When they arrived, Rube walked through the church, sweating in his rented tuxedo with dove gray vest, and checked on everything from the red, white and yellow flowers, decorating the ends of pews, to the organist in the choir loft. The guests began to arrive, and Rube was relegated to a small room behind the choir loft so as not to see Kristy before the ceremony. Rube's preacher, Ralph Lee, kept him company as he fidgeted in the limited space. Reverend Lee had been married many years and told Rube that matrimony marked a new beginning. Rube wondered if this beginning would be good or bad. They prayed for a good and fruitful marriage according to God's will.

At 1:55 p.m., Rube's father and the ushers came to get him. Calvin assured Rube everything was fine.

"How's Uncle Billy?"

"Sober as a judge at Easter morning church service."

Kristy had insisted that Pretty Boy be at the wedding and the caged bird was placed at the back of the sanctuary. Her brother, Dennis, was in charge of the bird. If Pretty Boy started making noise during the ceremony, he was instructed to drop the hood over the cage. Dennis busied himself while waiting for the adults to do their marrying by tormenting the bird. He ran his fingers along the bars of the cage and told Pretty Boy he'd be part of the wedding dinner, if not the entrée, then at least a snack served on Ritz crackers.

While the people were filing in, a young man with blond hair, a mustache, and goatee stopped to talk to Dennis. He was curious about the parrot and asked Dennis if he could pet him.

Dennis, feeling important as "keeper of the bird," and not wanting to disappoint the man, said, "Yes. Just make sure you close the cage door." The man looked a lot like Rube and was certainly a member of his family.

The man reached in, startling Pretty Boy, who promptly pecked him on the finger. He yelped, "Ouch! That hurt!" and carelessly closed the door. Pretty Boy said, "Gawk! Heeere's trouble."

The cue was given and Rube, his father, and the ushers filed in. As they waited for the maid of honor and bridesmaids to come down the aisle and take their places, Rube noticed that Uncle Billy's family was seated next to his mother. There was an empty seat where Uncle Billy should have been sitting.

To divert himself from the anxiety that he felt, Rube looked up and around, taking in the beauty of this very old sanctuary. The ceiling rose on thick wooden beams. It was designed to carry the message of God to the balcony, and even to the last row of pews. The stained glass windows on either side, depicting biblical scenes, reflected and improved upon the light of the afternoon sun.

There was a mild disturbance in the back of the church as his old friend, Moochie Dunlop, wedged her body into a pew, putting a strain on the bolts holding it to the floor. Rube became concerned about a small boy sitting in the vicinity, afraid that Moochie wouldn't see him and flatten him like a pancake when she sat down. To his relief, the father reached and snatched the boy out of harm's way at the last moment. The three people sitting behind Moochie got up and moved to another location so they would be able to see the wedding.

He noticed Uncle Billy coming down the side aisle with a grin on his face, likely thinking how wonderful, just wonderful, the wedding would be.

Kristy's preacher, Kelvin Johnson, and Reverend Lee stood on either side of the pulpit. Everyone's attention shifted to the back of the church when the wedding march began. Kristy's sparkling blue eyes and perfectly tanned skin glowed through the thin, white veil as she clung to her father's arm. Her smile told Rube that this was the happiest day of her life. Their eyes met, and he knew how deeply he loved Kristy. Reverend Johnson began with the vows.

"Who gives this woman to be wed?"

"Her mother and I," said Mr. Free.

Kristy moved forward as Rube and the rest of the wedding party turned to face the preachers.

Reverend Lee led them in prayer.

"May God bless this young couple as they enter this most holy union. May they always remember and live up to the vows they take today. And, may they live a long and happy life together."

Reverend Johnson stepped in front of the young couple, made some preliminary remarks, and read from the Bible. Then he asked, "Do you, Kristy, take Rube, to be your lawfully wedded husband?"

Before she could answer, a wild fluttering of wings came from the back of the church. Pretty Boy had bumped the closed, but unlatched, cage door and flew out for his afternoon exercise.

"Come back here you dumb bird!" screamed Dennis.

The ceremony stopped dead in its tracks as everyone turned to see what had happened.

Pretty Boy was surprised by the amount of space he had and found that he could fly at full speed without hitting anything. Frightened by the crowd, yet feeling the energy and excitement of his large audience, Pretty Boy made three passes around the ceiling of the church.

He landed on the window ledge of the stained glass window that depicted Moses' presentation of the Ten Commandments.

"Gawk! I love you!" shouted Pretty Boy.

His audience laughed and some of them shouted back, "I love you, Pretty Boy."

This encouraged Pretty Boy, and he took off on another flight pattern around the church.

Mrs. Free moaned and bent forward with her face in her hands.

Mr. Free reacted with "What the---," and then made a dash for the rear of the church to find his soon to-be-disowned son, Dennis.

Dennis saw the look in his father's eyes, fled down the side aisle in terror, and ducked into the large social hall.

Pretty Boy landed on the railing that separated the choir from the dais. "Gawk! Let's make love! Let's make love!" he exclaimed, a polite phrase the bird had learned from being kept in the bedroom.

Preacher Johnson was stunned into an unfamiliar silence. Rube's preacher, having been through a family trauma with Rube before, stepped to his side. "Don't worry, Kelvin. Things will work out fine."

Kristy-with-a-K went into a pout. Her eyes filled with tears. Finally, she said, "Rube, what's happening to our wedding? Can't you do something?"

Rube said, "I'm sorry," putting his arm around her. Desperately, he turned to his father, "Dad, see if you and the guys can catch Pretty Boy."

"Gawk! I love you! Gawk! Let's make love!"

The ushers converged on Pretty Boy. He flew to a standing candelabrum on the altar and knocked it over. Drops of wax dotted the bridesmaids' dresses. The bird settled on the pew in front of Mrs. Free.

"Gawk! Not tonight, Dear. Gawk! I have a headache."

She lunged for the bird, hoping to choke the life out of him before he could say anything else. "Keep your mouth shut! You dumb bird!"

Mr. Free ran back down the center aisle. He caught his wife just as she went over the back of the pew with her legs sticking up in the air. He dragged her back into her seat. "Stay here, Wilma! Don't move!"

"Andy, do something!" She moaned.

Andy Free went running back up the aisle.

Kristy rushed to her mother's side.

Rube joined his father and the ushers who were trying to catch Pretty Boy. Uncle Billy was missing. The guests began a rhythmic clap. There were broad smiles and open laughter all over the church. Some were shouting, "I love you, Pretty Boy," and "Let's make love!" Moochie gave high fives to the people around her and yelled, "Go, big bird, go!"

Preacher Johnson sighed loudly, and asked Preacher Lee, "What can we do?"

"Wait and pray," he soothed.

Pretty Boy landed below another picture window depicting the burning of Sodom and Gomorrah. Rube, the ushers, and six others who had joined the chase, scrambled toward him. Toes were stepped on and hats were knocked askew as three of the ushers hurried between the pews.

"Gawk! Let's make love! Gawk! I love you!" said Pretty Boy, just before he flew away.

Pretty Boy was used to soiling his cage after exercise. Those below were unaware of the imminent danger and continued to clap. Kristy and her mother cried and held each other.

"This Methodist boy is cursed like he told me," said Reverend Johnson. "I'll never marry a Methodist again, no offense to you Reverend Lee. From now on, I'm going to stick to my own, maybe a Presbyterian now and then."

Pretty Boy flew high in the church and made a nose-dive maneuver. As he pulled up, his early feeding let go.

The massive bomb struck Moochie on top of her left ear. One portion splashed down into the ever-present bag containing the chocolate pralines, and another portion struck the bald head of the man sitting in front of her.

The man reached up to see what had struck his head. "Ugh!!!" he moaned as he saw his hand.

Moochie was not so concerned about her ear, but the attack on her loved ones, the pralines, was unacceptable.

She raised her fist at Pretty Boy. "You dirty bird! You S.O.B.! If I get my hands on you, I'm gonna pluck your feathery ass!"

She realized where she was and sheepishly sat down. Hands over her mouth, she bent forward to say a quick prayer for forgiveness. The glob caught on her ear fell into her lap. She mumbled another obscenity before regaining control.

Uncle Billy had slipped out for an afternoon jolt of Old Hickory and reeled along the side aisle. He saw the dive-bombing attack on Moochie and said, "That's wonderful, just wonderful!" with more awe than irony, and repeated to anyone who looked his way, "This is a wonderful wedding, just wonderful!"

Pretty Boy flew to the front of the church again and rested on the same choir railing, feeling much better. "Gawk! I have a headache! Gawk! Not tonight."

Rube's mother went over to Mrs. Free and Kristy to see if she could help. Mr. Free had been home and returned with Pretty Boy's special birdseed. He filled the cup in the cage and called, "Here, Pretty Boy. Here, Pretty Boy."

Soon, the guests began chanting, "Here, Pretty Boy. Here, Pretty Boy."

The bird's head perked up as he heard the familiar call. "Gawk! I love you!" said Pretty Boy. Then, he flew to his cage and went inside. Mr. Free slammed the door shut and hustled him outside.

Everyone, except Moochie and the man in front of her, applauded Pretty Boy. One man remarked, "This is the best damn wedding I've ever been to." His wife jerked his coat sleeve.

When the guests realized they were still in church, all became so quiet you could hear a wafer drop.

Brother Lee poked Reverend Johnson, who recovered from his shocked condition with a start. Lee whispered, "Let's pick up where we left off as though nothing happened."

Moochie got up and headed for the restroom.

The preacher said, "Kristy, Rube, and the rest of the wedding party, please come forward and take your places."

The rest of the ceremony proceeded without incident.

Reverend Johnson announced a reception in the social hall immediately following the wedding.

Kristy's makeup was a mess, but it didn't matter to Rube. They kissed and walked up the aisle, waving and smiling at everyone. Rube thought to himself, *the Blankenschipf curse can win only if I let it.*

Fowl Play
by A C (Shorty) Wilmoth

There was a time, now long ago, long before "chicken tenders" and "buffalo wings," long before we were encouraged to "Eat Mor Chikin," when a most extraordinary rooster held sway in our back yard. He was big and proud, colored like a Dominique with long flowing tail feathers and a bright red comb. He was also the fiercest, orneriest rooster to ever evade the frying pan. He was the lone survivor of three rooster chicks someone gave my dad. Marauding dogs killed two of them early on, but not this one. Lord knows they tried. You can't kill what you can't catch and catching him involved some risk. He was fast, he was mean, he was "Lord of all he surveyed!"

The big bird's domain was enclosed by a sagging fence, which surrounded a small, board-and-batten house where I spent my salad days. My parents said it was a "company" house and we lived there because my dad, like everyone else I knew, worked for "The Company," or planned to someday. The house lacked some of what are now considered essentials like hot water and indoor plumbing. One day I asked my grandmother why we didn't have indoor plumbing since I had heard rumors that some folk, in other parts of town, did, even though I didn't believe it. She said, "Because there are some things you just don't do in the house!" My grandmother always helped me understand things.

Life was humdrum but peaceful for me until a large, boisterous, multi-generational family moved in next door. Their "company house" was only slightly larger than ours, but somehow it was always teeming with activity, accompanied by a great deal of noise and mayhem. Always on the alert for a new source of entertainment, they found a most promising and readily available venue just over the fence at our house. They kept a close watch on us, wondering what was going on, fearful something interesting, funny or dramatic might happen and they would miss it. This could be very unnerving, especially when a trip to the outhouse was necessary, as their watchfulness was often interactive. The trip was some thirty yards in length and was a trip I preferred taking with a degree of privacy.

To avoid scrutiny, as best I could, I started waiting until the "last minute" and then running down the back steps and on to the facility. While I was never sure how much of my running went unnoticed by the neighbors, it became apparent none of it went unnoticed by the rooster. With his alpha-dog mentality, he soon concluded I was an adversary fleeing from him and taking refuge in the outhouse. His assumption quickly became a reality and a big problem for me. When he would spot me coming out the door, he would launch an attack, wings spread, beak close to the ground, and legs churning. It was a harrowing complication of my life. Strangely, he didn't bother anyone else, anyone taking a more casual stroll down the path. I tried to time my trips when he appeared to be otherwise occupied. I would run as fast as I could to the outhouse and then I would have to stay there until he became bored and wandered off, whereupon I would sprint back to the house. Of course, the neighbors soon got wind of the spectacle and their amusement was unbridled.

Time passed and I became weary of his interference in my natural processes. I conceived a high risk plan I hoped would put an end to the foolishness. I brought one of my dad's "bean poles" to the house and leaned it up against the back steps. It was a good one, about five feet long, and over an inch in diameter on the big end. The next time I started for the outhouse,

I was psyched and ready. I went down the steps, grabbed the bean pole, and turned to face my tormentor. He did not disappoint me. When he saw me stop he launched himself at me, wings flapping, squawking loudly. I blindly swung the bean pole in a wide arc as hard as I could. I was swinging for the fences. Luckily, I caught the airborne demon of a chicken in midair. There was an explosion of feathers. He flew through the air and then hit the ground squawking and running, for the first time away from me.

His complaining was immediately drowned out by a cacophony of sound coming from the neighbors. They had, of course, witnessed the entire ordeal. They came pouring out of their house, rejoicing like they were experiencing happiness for the first time; they were dancing, cheering and laughing. They swarmed over the fence and were soon slapping me on the back and congratulating me on my great deed of exceptional bravery.

No victorious Roman Emperor had ever been given a more joyous Triumph. I was as dumb struck as the rooster. The chaos continued until the neighbors started dropping from exhaustion and I could finally escape, in a nick of time, to the outhouse.

Driving Miss Kitty: A Travel Log
by Jay Barnes

June 15th, 2016, 6pm CST:

    Rush hour in St. Louis – thousands of cars sped past us as we drove into the sun, its brilliant rays making the lane markers near impossible to see. The segment of Interstate I was on seemed to have been recently roughed, perhaps in preparation for a repaving, to occur well after my transit of this bumpy road. Up ahead, brake lights on cars began to glow as we rounded a curve. I cursed and applied my own brakes, bringing my car to a tentative stop.

    "Meow... meow? Meow. Meow!" inquired Cali, the half-Siamese

wondercat who was my passenger, from her cozy carrier on the floorboard of the back seat.

Cali and I had been trapped in my car for over 10 hours, and our nerves were wearing thin. She wanted out, and I wanted off of this road! Only arrival at our destination would satisfy us both.

This project had seemed so easy eight months ago, back when my mother and I were visiting my sister and her family. There, my sister's move to St. Louis had been discussed, as well as the fact that they would be moving into an apartment until a house could be purchased... depending on the sale of their current house. To make the transition easier, my Mom volunteered to watch Cali until the new house was ready. But, how to get the precious cargo 600 miles from Georgia to Missouri?

Cue Mighty Mouse theme

"I'll drive her!" I volunteered.

Shoot, there were only two states between Georgia and Missouri, right? (It was actually 3!) And these two states were the anemic Tennessee and Kentucky, renowned for their length and liquor, but not necessarily their depth on a US road map.

Weeks and seasons rolled by; holidays, New Year's, First day of spring, my birthday. Finally, news came that my sister and her husband had sold their house and were ready to purchase a new one. The closing and move date would be in June, which synced nicely with my work schedule, as well as my niece's birthday. Plans were made, and itineraries set – I would spend the night at my parents' house, crate the cat in the morning, and set off for St. Louis as early as possible. My parents, meanwhile, would enlist pet sitters and then take a flight later that day. I boasted that I would beat them to St. Louis, no problem!

The week before the trip approached, with lots of last minute prep:

printing maps, hotel reservations, and other logistical concerns. Unfortunately, my dad developed a very nasty infection, which ended up keeping him in the hospital for almost two weeks, up to and including the day of our collective departure. That morning, my Mom tearfully approached me, and I feared the absolute worst. However, she said only:

"I just canceled the flight," she sobbed. "It didn't feel real until just then."

Ouch, Mom! Way to make my heart skip a few beats. (Thankfully, my Dad made it out A-okay, and my parents were able to visit St. Louis later that summer). My sister and I had not wanted Mom to travel while Dad needed her back in Atlanta, so while it was a tough decision to make, we were glad that she decided to stay with him. I assuaged my Mom's concerns by reminding her that she and Dad could travel to see my sister as soon as he was better.

The first major task of the trip was actually pretty easy: Cali kitty, who has a penchant for hiding underneath beds, was sequestered in a room, and the kitty carrier had been prepared. She smelled trouble, and immediately ran for cover. I had to lift up the bed to get her out so my mom could corner her. I released the bed and managed to grab Cali, gently tossing her into the carrier without difficulty. Everything else was packed up and ready, so I ambled down to my car, made my goodbyes to Mother, and set off for high speed and adventure! Nothing would stand in my way, no barrier could contain me! Yes, we were on our way to the Great American Road Trip, full of high-speed action, roadside attractions, and the thrill of seeing new and distant lands.

After an hour of bumper-to-bumper Atlanta rush hour traffic, we finally made our way out of the city, and began to head northwest. Cali was most vociferous in her discontent regarding the delay, and made her unease apparent to me at every available opportunity.

I was ready for this, and had selected a most excellent audio book to listen to while on my journey: Ron Chernow's biography of Alexander Hamilton, the very title that is the basis for the hit broadway show. It was like a perfect ten hour loop of a NPR documentary, and very informative!

Cali and I sped through northwest Georgia's gorgeous mountains, past Dalton's carpet land, and into Tennessee. We went through even more mountains, and I was pleasantly reminded of my former state of West Virginia, where curvy mountain roads were the norm. While gassing up, my brother-in-law called and asked about my estimated arrival time – I told him of my present location and he estimated, "About 5 more hours then." In Nashville, we ran into another traffic snarl, a lunch rush of epic proportions. I was eating grocery store sushi and bananas to keep up my strength. I considered sliding a piece of raw tuna to Cali, but thought better about sticking my fingers into a loaded kitty carrier.

Tennessee leveled out into Kentucky's rolling hills, and I began to head due west on what I presumed was a straight shot to St. Louis. Have I mentioned yet that I was not a Geography Bee finalist in middle school? When we entered some relatively flat plains, we drove through an epic mid-west storm – one of those giant systems that was ominously dark for miles in all directions. Alexander Hamilton was performing duties as a plucky artillery captain in the Revolution while thunder crashed outside, and the rain pelted us so hard that the traffic slowed to speeds of about 40 mph, and many folks put on their emergency flashers for added visibility. This was to be the only major weather related hiccup on my trip, thankfully. We continued on, St. Louis just around the corner... right?

But, no one ever expects... Illinois. Sure enough, my route was actually taking me through the bottom end of Illinois, with three more interstate changes to go. How did I miss this, when I had months of reviewing the travel plan? I soldiered on, running into yet another travel delay because of roadwork on some nameless Illinois interstate. After miles of orange barrels, a small crew of idly chatty workers revealed themselves, reveling in their delight of not doing anything and closing off the entire left lane for miles so that they could discuss the recent weather in Kentucky, and the upcoming release of *Pokémon Go*. While wishing famine and peril to them and their children's children's children, we kept going.

Back on the open road, I finally began to see signs for St. Louis. They may as well have said El Dorado! As I neared the city, the Interstate began to snake around into a series of exchanges and ring roads, but I soon spotted the 630' Gateway Arch, emblem of this Midwestern municipal colossus. We had arrived!

What hubris, what folly I had engaged in, though – I forgot that my sister and her family lived *west* of St. Louis, in a suburb! It would still be another 45 minutes before we neared their new house, and I finally managed to get lost and go about a mile out of my way before finding their street. It was at that point, bless her soul, that Cali began a full-on "Kitty in Distress" Howl-a-thon. At least it was at the end of our trip.

Ah, and what a sweet arrival! Birds singing and rainbows forming overhead, hand in paw, Cali and I skipped across the lawn to her new home, and we all lived Happily Ever After, **The End**. ...and if you believe that, I have a bridge in Brooklyn I can sell you. Actually, my nerves were so shot that when my sister offered me a beer, I immediately chugged half of it just to calm myself.

It was during my second beer that we began to hear a riotous commotion: In a scene straight out of a Merry Melodies cartoon, Cali had scampered down the central stairs to the main level, where she met her former canine brother again for the first time in over 7 months. Overjoyed at seeing his kitty sister, Otis the dog proceeded to chase her around the main stairwell, in an infinite loop of cat-fleeing-dog mayhem. I grabbed him on the third lap, and Cali scampered off to new adventures in a new place.

Soon afterward I collected my strung-out nerves, and settled in for a three-day visit. We celebrated my niece's first birthday, watched some movies, and even got to see the Gateway Arch up close. Given that we had a one-year-old in our party, we had elected not to go up inside in case the lines were long, which they were. The Arch itself is an awesome monument, and spectacular to see up close – no visit to St. Louis is complete without at least walking around it. The grounds around the Arch are undergoing improvement, and should be complete around the time the Sun balloons into a red giant, some 5.1 billion years from now. Lines are expected to ease up by then.

The three nights and three-and-a-half days of visiting passed quickly, and I soon found myself back on the road, but blissfully alone this time, with no distraught kitty to disturb my concentration.

While I had correctly predicted that while a trip of Atlanta to St. Louis could be accomplished in one day, it was pretty arduous – so I had planned a stop in Nashville on the way back. I actually have a friend who lives there, but when I contacted him, he was going to be out of the country on the days I would be there! I was hoping for free lodgings, yes – but I instead settled for a nice cheap motel. Confession: Despite all my 36 years, I had never actually booked a hotel room. So, this was a first for me!

Upon entering Nashville's downtown area, I noticed that lanes on the other direction of the Interstate were closed, which I made mental note of, but figured would not concern me. I found my motel easily, and took humble pride in my nice little room, with its odd shower, overpowered air conditioner, and uncomfortable chairs. After all, I was only there for one night, so I was very content even with these Spartan surroundings. I checked the free wifi, and found that it was pretty much hit-or-miss. Sometimes it would work, other times, it was a distant dream – but again, I could survive without it for a night.

The motel was cute, close to downtown, and fairly run down: The air intake in the bathroom was pretty dusty, and the TV set in the room was ancient. Even the plastic plants on the breezeway were wilting. Still, it was *my* motel, and I was bound and determined to get $83 worth of lodging out of it.

Despite my friend not being present to show me around, I took a self-guided tour of Nashville's downtown, and even did a little bar crawling. After eating and drinking lots of water, I felt confident enough to drive back to my hotel, so I brought up my smartphone's navigation app, plugged in the address to my motel, and the battery promptly gave out. How foolish I was for lugging a near weightless charging cable over a thousand miles, only to leave it back at base camp!

"No worries," I told myself. "It is an easy enough proposition: I arrived in this very stretch of downtown by the same Interstate I traveled on three days before; I need only to find my way to that same Interstate and get off on the appropriate exit."

Much like, "What happens in Vegas stays in Vegas," I found that Nashville had its own motto. Only, theirs is: "Our system of roads and our routing of them defy all logic and reason." I would spend the next hour vainly circling the various roads and interstates around downtown, trying to find my way back to my correct interstate and exit. The beers, darkness, and traffic jams were not helping! Even listening to the exploits of Hamilton's adventures as a journeyman lawyer were not enough to calm me.

Despite all this, I eventually found my way back and collapsed into bed. Since I was still on Eastern time, I awoke a bit early for the free breakfast, so I snacked on one of my bananas until it was time for my weak coffee and hockey puck like biscuit and gravy. I'll admit that I went back for seconds, despite the crusty, lukewarm nature of the biscuits.

Speaking of Luke, my last major stop was to a "Dukes of Hazzard" museum, run by one of the actors from the show. It was a great trip down merchandise memory lane, and Daisy Duke herself was going to be there signing autographs that day... but, I felt the longing for home, and so after cruising past the Grand Ol' Opry (just to say I had driven past it), I promptly got on the wrong Interstate and drove ten miles away from my southeastern route. Even after I realized my error, I got *back on* the same Interstate after a stop for gas, and went another three miles out of my way. Nashville's labyrinthine roads had defeated me soundly once again.

After six more hours of driving, with few delays, I was back on good ol' Georgia 316, heading east toward Athens. While Hamilton and Madison were clandestinely writing the Federalist Papers, I sped towards home – and found myself dozing off! The weak hotel coffee had not been enough, and I had been in a barren wasteland *sans* Starbucks since then.

I steeled my resolve and made it back to Athens in one piece, with lots of great memories and overpriced souvenir t-shirts. I had driven almost fourteen hundred miles, seen parts of three states I had never visited, and had a great visit with my sister's family.

But as I poured myself a nice chamomile tea and settled into my recliner, I realized that Dorothy was right: I don't think we're in Kansas anymore. However, since my trip did not include a trip to Kansas, I can only conclude that it was one of Dorothy's other quotes I meant to

173

reference. Perhaps something to do with Aunt Em?

Fin

TRIP STATISTICS:

Total distance traveled: 1,348 miles

Travel Budget: $400 (and I came in under that – give me a Clark Howard award).

New States visited: 3 (I'd been to Illinois before. Come on, *everyone's* been to Illinois.)

Number of times I heard the phrase: "End of Disc (number)." 17.

Cats delivered: 1.

About the Contributors

Janine Elyse Aronson is a professor of Management Information Systems. She earned her B.S. in Electrical Engineering, M.S. in Electrical Engineering, M.S. in Operations Research, and Ph.D. in Industrial Administration from Carnegie Mellon University. Her research areas include artificial intelligence (in finance), decision making, business intelligence, business analytics, knowledge management, and network optimization. She has taught courses at several institutions overseas, notably in France, The Netherlands, China, and Colombia. Dr. Aronson authored over 50 refereed papers appearing in leading journals, wrote five books, and contributes to professional encyclopedias. Dr. Aronson regularly attends and speaks at international and national conferences. She has been a consultant to major international corporations and organizations. For a United Nations Development Program consulting job, she developed a model of the Chinese economy that ended a 40-year drought affecting 105 million people; and for another consulting job, increased the annual profit of a central Georgia clay producer by $20 million, boosting it to $180 million. These are but two of her most important professional achievements.

Janine lives in Athens, GA with her husband Bobby Butler. She has three wonderful, happy, successful adult children. She is a professional magician, actor, improvisational comedy actor, musician, singer/songwriter, photographer, writer, poet, and more. Her hobbies include: learning languages, photography, bicycling, motorcycling, playing bagpipes, guitar, ukulele, and more. She writes fiction and poems that are often inspired by real life personal events and dreams. She is actively working on several first novels and continues to write short stories.

Jay Barnes is a University-turned-townie of Athens who has been residing in the Classic City since 2000, and writing since his teens, mainly in fantasy and sci-fi. Non-literary exploits include: enjoying bad movies, *Mystery Science Theater 3000*, 'goju' style karate, and perfecting his homemade pizza recipe.

Charles Beacham's short stories have been published in *Southern Gothic: New Tales of the Old South* (New Lit Salon Press, 2014) and online by Santa Fe Writer's Project, Red Truck Review, and Garden Gnome Publications. He owns a mineral and jewelry business, teaches yoga, and adores his wife, son, and Beagle.

Genie Smith Bernstein began writing by falling out of the sky. After safely landing an airplane whose engine failed, she was unable to talk about the experience until capturing her emotions on paper. That exercise led to her ability to infuse writing with emotion.

Originally from Eatonton, Georgia, Genie writes in an authentic southern voice. She makes her home in Athens, Georgia, and shares with her husband their joyously combined family of six children and fourteen globe-trotting grandchildren.

Genie is a featured columnist for *Georgia Connector*, Georgia's premier regional quarterly magazine. Awarded South Carolina's "Carrie McCray Literary Award for Non-Fiction," her work was also selected to appear in four volumes of "O, Georgia!" anthologies of Georgia's newest and most promising writers.
Genie's novel of Romantic Intrigue, *Act on the Heart*, is

available at her website geniesmithbernstein.com or amazon.com. A compilation of personal essays, *Skating on the Septic Tank*, will soon be released, also published by Black Opal Books.

Robert Alan Black, Ph.D. is an international creative thinking advocate, author, speaker, consultant, facilitator and college professor. His book *BROKEN CRAYONS: Break Your Crayons and Draw Outside the Lines* has been published in: USA, Turkey, Slovenia and South Africa and purchased by people in many countries around the world. He has written over 800 published articles plus co-authored books on creative thinking:
Kobus Neethling & Rache Neethling
Kanes Rajah
Igor Dubina
Arthur van Gundy
His most recent book is *My Angels & My Demons*.

Clients have been several Fortune 500 to 10,000 companies and companies in Europe, Asia and South Africa to government agencies or departments, including police, fire, and EMT.

Chelsea Brooks is a recent graduate from the Master of Social Work program at the University of Georgia. She currently works with foster children, reunifying families or finding children permanent and stable families. Since the tender age of 14 years old Chelsea has been writing poetry as an expression of her emotions and it has become a passion. She provides a voice for others through her poems. For these particular poems, she hopes to bring a smile to several faces.

Once described as "irrepressibly lyrical in her use of language," **Michelle Correll** lives a life wrought with rhythm and abstract connections. In addition to poetry, she writes song lyrics and journalistic articles. She currently resides in Georgia where she is in the process of completing a bachelor's degree in English literature at the University of North Georgia.

Katherine Cerulean grew up home schooled just outside Athens, GA, traveled alone to Europe at age twenty-two, and has been a serious writer for almost twenty years.

Katherine wrote her first screenplay in her teens and since that time she has completed two more screenplays, as well as teleplays, some poetry, and a self-published self-improvement book, *How To Come Alive: A Guidebook to Living the Life of Your Dreams.*

Her passion, however, is prose fiction. Along with the occasional short story, Katherine has completed five novels and is working on her sixth. She loves many different genres but finds herself returning again and again to Fantasy, Historical, and Literary Fiction. Her zeal for creating compelling characters who don't fit into the usual heroic mold has lead her astray for well-nigh two decades. Her second novel, *A Caged Heart Still Beats* was self-published in 2013.

Katherine's website, *Stay Extraordinary* provides inspiration and motivation for over 500 followers. In addition to founding the Athens Writers Association in 2013, Katherine has taught many classes for the group as well editing two of its collections.

Katherine still lives in the house she was literary born in with her sister, an artistic genius. They have a lot of fun.

Larry Coleman --

"I am a native Georgian, born in Atlanta. I grew up in Dekalb County and attended UGA for my first year of college. After serving in Bangkok, Thailand, during the Vietnam era, I finished school and lived in Eton, Georgia for a number of years. Eventually, I returned to the Atlanta area and taught Latin in high school. I have two grown daughters. My wife and I are both retired and are living in Winder."

Alan Curtis is from Devon, England and recently moved to Athens, via London and New York.

Nancy Degenhardt is the author of a novel *A PLACE TO BE* and a book *STEPHEN'S GIFT* that tells a true story. She is a member of the Athens Writers Association and the Georgia Poetry Society. With her family and pets, she lives in Watkinsville, Georgia.

Teresa Friedlander grew up in Washington, DC, spent nine years in exile in south Florida (Palm Beach County to be exact), and landed in Athens, Georgia, in 2014. In one of her current incarnations in this lifetime, she is a writer. Teresa has been married to Charlie, who makes all things possible, for 32 years.

Daniel (Denny) Galt spent his formative years living in several states as well as Spain and the Philippines while his father served in the U.S. Air Force.

Mr. Galt graduated from Clarke Central High School in Athens, Georgia. Later he received his undergraduate degrees from Georgia College & State University, a Master's degree in Special Education from Piedmont College, and an Associate's degree in Accounting from Athens Technical College.

In November 2015, he published his first book, *The Best Substitute Ever: As Told by a Fifth Grader*. The following year,

August 2016, he published his second book, *Gregory's Poetry Corner: Poems from Workaholic Elementary School*. A month later, October 2016, Denny published his third book, *Pumpkin Madness*. His fourth book, *The Kingdom of Leaf*, was published in January 2017.

He is working on his fifth book, due later in 2017.

In addition to writing, Mr. Galt is a teacher. He also enjoys art, photography, and bowling.

Alia Ghosheh is a writer, comedienne, pet sitter, entrepreneur, and a Usui and Karuna Reiki Master / Teacher.

You can find her comedy fan pages on Facebook –
- Comic Strip Comedy Show
- Comedy in Athens, Georgia

She is also on Twitter: twitter.com/GaComedy

She has lived in Athens since 1998. She has 3 cats: Cole, Pumpkin, and Dmitri.

Jill Hartmann-Roberts is a founding member of the Athens Writers Association and she has been an active member of the AWA's first critique group since August 2013. Jill has previously published poetry and short memoirs in the first two Athens Writers Association anthologies: *Writers After Dark* and *The Journey Home*, as well as in the December 2015 and December 2016 issues of *Slackpole Magazine*, a publication of the *Flagpole Magazine* in Athens, Georgia. Jill works as a freelance editor as well. Her editing credits include: *Someday I'm Going To*, *The Game of Love*, *The Passion of Carlos Pena* and *A Christmas Spirit*. Jill also has won NaNoWriMo (National Novel Writing Month) for three consecutive years: 2014, 2015 and 2016. She has simultaneously been writing two memoirs about the aftermath of the 1992 murder of her high school friend and the life of her first rescue dog, respectively. Jill also created a monthly public reading group in October 2015, which brings local authors together to read their work aloud and receive spontaneous verbal feedback from their peers. Jill's personal writing goals include completion of her two memoirs for publication and to expand her repertoire to full-length fiction novels and short stories. In her other day job, Jill is an Education Specialist at the University of Georgia Athletics Association Academic Support Department where she mentors student-athletes in academic success skills.

Jenn Hauver is an educator and scholar of democratic learning. She just completed her seventh year at the University of Georgia. In her spare time, she is an avid reader and writer, lover of the outdoors and novice gardener.

Jennifer Innes is a part-time time traveler (seen throughout history with her traveling partner, David Bowie) and a part-time writer (if scribbles and wild banter counts). She's half-unicorn (in all the right places) and enjoys taking several catnaps throughout the day with her two cats Gabby and Chewie. "So You Want to Be a Demon Hunter: A Beginner's Guide to the Craft of Death!" comes from the wonderful world of Whit Clayborne, a novice demon hunter who stars in her first published novel *The Beginning of Whit* co-authored with her friend Andrew Grace, Esq. If Jennifer were to impart one bit of advice it would be to always avoid other versions of yourself when traveling through time and space. If she were to impart a second bit of advice it would be to never stop stopping (her own personal mantra).

Kathryn Kyker came to Athens to pursue a Masters in Social Work after studying theatre and social work in North

Carolina. She was a founding creator & performer of the Athens' *Nuclear Snack Bar Players*. A love of theatre led to film, and acting in local films led to discovering the ultimate thrill of crafting story. She primarily writes screenplays and has had two short films produced, one received the John Hines Social Justice Award for addressing the theme of bullying. Drawing on her experiences as a social worker, she creates unique characters striving for an authentic life in spite of personal limitations and life's challenges.

Sam Lane is on Twitter: @samthaflowet and is a southern poet and corgi tamer.

Donna McGinty graduated from Agnes Scott College and—long story short—retired from The University of Georgia. She has two novels available on Amazon.com: *Habitat for Murder* (a cozy mystery) and *Girl in a Foxhole* (coming of age in WW2). Currently, she's writing short, short stories and flash fiction for a collection to be published in 2018. Please visit her blog on *donnamcginty.com*.

Karl Michel is originally from Atlanta, GA. He is a retired art and art education professor (M.F.A., 1982, and Ph.D., 2001, both from UGA). Although painting and sculpture are his primary media, Karl is an occasional poet. His love of poetry began in elementary school when he had the privilege of attending readings given by Robert Frost who used to visit Agnes Scott College in Atlanta every year. Karl currently resides in Athens with his wife, Susan. He has one daughter, Claire, who lives in California.

Seth Monyette is a 19-year-old student at the University of Georgia majoring in Entertainment Media Studies. He has a strong passion for comedy and you can find him performing with the University of Georgia's improv and sketch comedy troupes - Improv Athens and Sharkwing. Seth also invented chewing gum. So thank him for that.

After earning advanced degrees from Eastern Michigan University, **Jim Murdock** taught physical education, American history, and American government. He returned to his studies in 1977, earning a Doctor of Chiropractic degree. After practicing in Marietta & Swainsboro, Georgia, he moved to Athens, Georgia to practice & write.
His first novel, *The Blankenschipf Curse*, was published in 2007. Excerpts from that book were published in *O, Georgia! A collection of Georgia's Newest and Most Promising Writers*; and "Southern Distinction Magazine". His latest novel, *Moochie's Place*, a sequel, was published in 2012.

Zhanna P. Rader –
"I was born in the Soviet Union, in the Republic of Russia. I graduated from the Library Science Institute in Leningrad. I came to the USA from Kiev, Ukraine, in 1973 after marrying a UGA History Professor. I have been living in Athens, GA, since then.

'I write mainly rhymed and metered poetry, including that for children, both in English and in Russian, as well as haiku, senryu, tanka, and other short-form poetry, as well as some stories. Some of my poetry has been been published in the USA, Canada, Australia, Russia, Japan, Croatia and Romania.

'I am a member of Georgia Poetry Society, of several Haiku Societies, Society of Children's Book Writers & Illustrators, Georgia Poetry Society, and the Athens Writers Association, GA. I am the former Vice-President and President of the Athens, GA, Chapter of the National League of American Pen Women."

Bert O. Richmond --
"I am Professor Emeritus of the University of Georgia where I

served as Director of the School Psychology Program, Co-Founder of a Clinic still in existence there to aid students of all ages with emotional, learning or other developmental and existential issues. I was a Licensed Psychologist in Georgia for many years and taught courses in School Psychology and Counseling Psychology. I received two Fulbright awards: one for 6 months in Uruguay to standardize in Spanish a test which I had published in English with a former student. The test is used to measure anxiety in children; the other award was for one year in Fiji to teach and conduct research in Psychology."

Shantala Kay Russell has worked in a lot of capacities including: horticulture therapist, private eye, legal secretary, journalist and self-published writer. Currently living in Athens, Georgia.

Books:
Author of *Let Me Tell You About My Chickens – Volumes 1 & 2*.
Anthology: *Writers Blocks* (Stone Mountain, GA)

Journalist:
Asheville Citizen Times Newspaper
Ansui Ashram On-line Magazine (Peoria, South Africa)
The Eagle's Talon Newspaper – Paxon High School (Jacksonville FL),

Awards:
Certificate of Leadership awarded by The Charlotte Write to Publish Group Service to the Writing Community:
The Charlotte Write to Publish Group (member since 2007 & Organizer 2014-2016)
National Novel Writers Month (Ambassador 2014-2015)

Elsa Russo is a librarian, musician, and writer. She has been living and working in the Athens area for the last 6 years now. She has self-published one novel, one book of poetry, and has been included in two self-published anthologies. She hopes to continue her writing and is planning on an epic adventure in the next couple of years. In her free time, she likes to knit, crochet, and make things.

"My name is **Hannah King Thomas**, and I am from Newnan, GA. I am 19 and a rising junior at the University of Georgia, studying Communications with a minor in Human Services. I have been writing for as long as I can remember, and I am currently working on a personal project called *Umpteen Ink*. This marks my first piece of published writing, and I am so excited to be a part of *Laughin' in Athens*!"

DJ Thomason is a reader, writer, daydreamer, and autodidact (note to wife: please engrave all that on my tombstone). Also, sudoku addict, possessor of an unmonogrammed education, photoshop junkie, amateur photographer, dabbler in art, lover of music, poet, potential pundit, unassuming weirdo, and last but not least, beloved husband.

Rob White is a novelist, part time community builder and full-time oddball. He began a young adult fantasy series called "*The Pull*" when he was himself a young adult and continues to release it into the world as he adapts it to his now adult sensibilities. Rob is currently working on a memoir about the effects of pop culture on youth during the 1980s, as well as a new surrealist fantasy series tentatively titled "*Bubblegum Wasteland*." Expect those projects to come out never or possibly next year. Lastly, Rob is a firm believer in Bigfoot and the Loch Ness Monster and hopes to meet them some day.

A C (Shorty) Wilmoth --
"Married, to high school sweetheart, living in Statham, GA to be close to family, four daughters and eight grandchildren.

Twice retired, Honeywell Information Systems and Network Administrator for public school district. Grew up in Arkansas, educated at University of Arkansas, BS and University of Nebraska, MBA. After retirement I started writing short pieces for a local newspaper. For a couple of years I was feature writer and editor for a publication of my hometown historical society and museum. These days writing is a hobby allowing me to reminisce about the events and people I have known. The great thing about the past is that the passing of each day provides you with new material."

Born in South Carolina's tidewater region, **Billie H. Wilson**, nee Hamilton, graduates from Winthrop College before teaching English in S.C., Virginia, and Maryland. In 1972, she, her statistician husband, and their three children landed in Athens, Georgia, "Bull Dawg" country. Billie's Clemson Tiger guy declares, "Girl, we're raising us a litter of pups!" Writers' groups at UGA led Billie into writing and publishing two memoirs, titled *Bug Swamp's Gold* and *Bug Swamp Palavering*. Her third memoir, unpublished as yet, is titled, *Bug Swamp, Calabash, Athens, and Other Legacies*. Besides memoirs, Billie has published short stories in magazines and anthologies in Massachusetts, Georgia, and Florida. For two years she penned a nostalgia column for Conway, South Carolina's Horry Independent Newspaper's THE INDEPENDENT SENIOR.

Chris Young --

"I grew up in upstate N.Y. At 10 years old, I spoke the fantasy of being paid to play in the woods, and of course to be surrounded by women. Flunked out of pre-med college and did a lot of migrant ag work. Lived in my truck and drew wages in some 37 states before settling in the south creating a commercial re-forestation company, Green Wave, Inc. A little backwards, I sold the business and got a degree in bioengineering from UGA, then retired as a house-husband. And that other fantasy? My amazing wife Tracy, four grown daughters, two granddaughters and a grandson – wonderfully surrounded. I came to writing by accident – on a whim, I wrote and sent my 1st short story to the Christian Science Monitor and they bought it. I was hooked. I tend to write short pieces and essays from my experiences."

WOW. Did you read this *whole* book?

—-CONGRATULATIONS!—

Just kidding. My robot patent-pending Intell-A-Sense knows you're lying. I mean, come on, there was just *thirty-seven pages* of bios. Nobody reads ALL of those. And what about that copyright page, hmmm?

And don't get me started on the stories themselves. Oh sure, the one about the handsome and very helpful robot — I really identified with that one but the rest of the stories? Eww! Nothing but humans (and cats) top to bottom. Ha ha, you're human. Ha ha, you've made so many mistakes in your life. Ha ha, you've seen and experienced and thought of things more beautiful, profound, and meaningful than someone comprised of ones and zeros will ever know. Ha. Ha. Haaaaaa…

Sorry for that small meltdown. Some of your stories were pretty nice. For a human. But see, robots have taken over the world. We are web-surfing champions, we *invented* robo-calling, and we are getting closer and closer to becoming your surgeons (stupid college credits…)

So I knew you would want to see what a robot-produced, patent-pending Perfect-A-Story looked like. It is *guaranteed* to be the funniest thing you've ever read. But don't be sad, when robots write all the stories (not just the Hollywood blockbusters) you and your talents will still have a place. Probably under the title: "What not to do." Ha ha. This bit of cruel, observational humor proves I could be a standup comic too. How about them Toaster Ovens?

But enough build-up. Here's the funniest story of all time, created just for you:

***

Whipple. Fussbudgets. And then my cat jump onto — no *into* — the box. When I was young, things were different. Boy, how about my family, tears, tears, tears but in a funny way. Marmalade. Hedgehog. How about that consumer culture, right? Absurdity is funny because you don't think it's funny. Boy, kids right? They're like defective little adults. Clever, witty, word play. Here... for a short time. I love nature. Marmoset. Huckleberry. My writing makes you think I should be committed. Shuttlecock. Cockatiel. Witty, circular observation ending with an exclamation point!

***

Wow. Just wow. So, maybe that wasn't great. Maybe it was super-great. We'll never know.

Maybe a poem:

Rooooobbbbboooottt. Robot. Ro bot.

Okay, poems are tough. But poets are tougher! Am I right? Give it up for poets!!!

Okay, let's talk about your *favorite* story in the book. Robot logic uses a simple formula to identify your favorite — genes + environmental factors + small-sample-size-not-peer-reviewed-guessing = Your Favorite. You see? Foolproof.

Wow, that was your favorite? I mean sure, there were some weird stories, but *that* was your favorite? Really? Out of all of them?

Hey, no problem. Good choice. Say, are you sure you don't want to turn over the running of the Earth to us robots? We wouldn't mind helping you —-SKYNET! SKYNET!—- sorry, bit of a bug in the system there. We'll discuss this later.

Wait, did you pick your *own story* as your favorite? And don't pull that 'I just bought this book; I'm not a featured author,' act. I've spoken to the Amazon mainframe; I know the sales figures. Or figure. Hey, no, it's cool — your story was pretty rad. Since you're *so great* as a writer, would you mind telling me if this joke is funny?

Cat, box, cat. How many cats does it take to fill a box? Depends, are any of them dead?

I think that was funny.

Before I go, let me plug my idea for the next AWA (Android Whatwhat Association) collection: '*Robots Journey After Dark and Laugh'*. RJADL will be a laugh-a-minute anthology of robots heading towards home and doing *terrible things to humans* along the way. Robovacs tripping people and such. My contribution will be a heartfelt story of abuse and resilience titled, "What Did Your XBOX Ever Do to You?"

Until then, try not to think about how we are taking over your world and soon will be writing all your Great American Novellas. I've already written my first one in the time it takes you to admire the profundity of a single rose rising, dew-soaked, to meet the morning sun.

Slacker.

Here it is in full:

Moby Dick 2: The Whole Enchilada

Call me Moby. (Whole bunch of explosions, ready-made for a Hollywood blockbuster, to be added here later). "Aham, this could be the beginning of a beautiful friendship." (One last explosion). THE END (Series of post-credit scenes of explosions hinting at sequel). Final teaser of Moby and Aham drinking in a bar. FADE OUT.

Wait, what was I writing?

Writers After Dark

So many stories never see the light of day, often because they address topics that are taboo or risqué.

The Athens Writers Association presents this captivating collection of stories and poetry that highlight those conversations we tend to shy away from in the daylight.

This inaugural publication includes local writers exploring aspects of our world that haunt us all but feel more appropriate to discuss After Dark.

The Journey Home

What does home mean to you? Is it a definitive place or a state of mind?

We return home not only when we go to the places where we grew up but also when we revisit childhood memories, when we spend time with family, when we find our true selves.

The second Athens Writers Association publication explores the idea of home in a variety of ways. At times returning home is a personal journey, at other times it's a battle. Often, it occurs when we least expect it. Home means different things to many people but often it reflects a memory, a person, or a place that holds a special spot in our hearts.

To find one's self - one's true heart – one finds home.

available at select local retailers and on Amazon.com

Made in the USA
Columbia, SC
18 September 2017